Merritt, Richard and Elizabeth Hanson
<u>Science, Politics, and Internatl Conferences</u>

SCIENCE, POLITICS, AND INTERNATIONAL CONFERENCES

Monograph Series in World Affairs
Graduate School of International Studies
University of Denver

Series Editor
Karen A. Feste, *University of Denver*

Editorial Board

Steven Brams
New York University

James Caporaso
University of Denver

Jerome Clubb
University of Michigan

Catherine Kelleher
University of Maryland

Robert Jervis
Columbia University

Michael O'Leary
Syracuse University

Todd Sandler
Iowa State University

Susan Strange
*London School of Economics
and Political Science*

Kenneth Thompson
University of Virginia

John Turner
University of Minnesota

Dina Zinnes
University of Illinois

New Books in the Series

- Exploring the Stability of Deterrence
  edited by Jacek Kugler and Frank C. Zagare

- Arms Transfers to the Third World: Probability Models of Superpower Decisionmaking   *Gregory S. Sanjian*

- Nigeria and the International Capitalist System
  edited by Toyin Falola and Julius Ihonvbere

- Defining Political Development
  Stephen Chilton

- Science, Politics, and International Conferences: A Functional Analysis of the Moscow Political Science Congress   *Richard L. Merritt and Elizabeth C. Hanson*

SCIENCE, POLITICS, AND INTERNATIONAL CONFERENCES

A Functional Analysis of the Moscow Political Science Congress

Richard L. Merritt
Elizabeth C. Hanson

GSIS Monograph Series
in World Affairs

THE UNIVERSITY OF DENVER

Lynne Rienner Publishers • Boulder & London

Published in the United States of America in 1989 by
Lynne Rienner Publishers, Inc.
1800 30th Street, Boulder, Colorado 80301

and in the United Kingdom by
Lynne Rienner Publishers, Inc.
3 Henrietta Street, Covent Garden, London WC2E 8LU

©1989 by Lynne Rienner Publishers, Inc. All rights reserved

Library of Congress Cataloging-in-Publication Data

Merritt, Richard L.
    Science, politics, and international conferences : a functional analysis of the Moscow Political Science Congress / by Richard L. Merritt and Elizabeth C. Hanson.
    Bibliography: p.
    Includes index.
    ISBN 1-55587-134-8 (alk. paper)
    1. International Political Science Association. World Congress (11th : 1979 : Moscow, R.S.F.S.R.)—Cost effectiveness.
2. Political science—Congresses—Cost effectiveness. I. Hanson, Elizabeth C. II. International Political Science Association. World Congress (11th : 1979 : Moscow, R.S.F.S.R.) III. Title.
JA35.5.I77   1979z   88-18322
320'.06'01—dc19   CIP

British Library Cataloguing in Publication Data
A Cataloguing in Publication record for this book
is available from the British Library.

Printed and bound in the United States of America

The paper used in this publication meets
the requirements of the American National
Standard for Permanence of Paper for
Printed Library Materials Z39.48-1984.

Dedicated to:

Liette Boucher
Karl W. Deutsch
Georgii Shakhnazarov
William Smirnov
John E. Trent

who made the Moscow World Congress work.

Contents

	List of Tables and Figures	ix
	Preface	xi
1	International Scientific Congresses: A Functional Approach	1
	The Scientific Consociation	3
	Growth of International Science	4
	Functions of International Scientific Congresses	9
	Perceptions and Realities: A Design for Research	19
2	International Political Science: From Paris to Moscow (and Back)	29
	Internationalization	30
	Politics of Site Selection	36
	Some Questions for Research	47
3	Who Went to Moscow and Why?	57
	Profile of Respondents	57
	Why Attend Professional Meetings?	63
	Value of International Scientific Congresses	64
	Deciding to Go to Moscow	72
4	An Occasion for Learning	77
	Expectations and Experiences	78
	Soviet Government and People	84

	International Scientific Networking	87
	Modifications in Scholarly Behavior	90
	Improving Scientific Communication at World Congresses	93
	Individual Learning	96
5	**Politics at Play**	**101**
	To Go to Moscow or Stay Home?	102
	Decisionmaking About Sites	106
	Politics on the Floor	112
	Impact of Politics	114
6	**Functions of International Scientific Congresses**	**119**
	Individual Political Scientists	119
	Research Organizations	124
	Scientific Associations	124
	Political Functions	127
	Some Future Directions	132

Appendix A Breakdown of Registrants by Country	143
Appendix B Questionnaires	145
1. Questionnaire for Registrants	145
2. Questionnaire for Nonregistrants	161
Appendix C Scales of Professionalism and Internationalism	169
Bibliography	175
Index	181
About the Book and the Authors	185

Tables and Figures

Tables

1.1	Growth and Geographical Distribution of International Meetings, 1950-1983	8
1.2	Size and Composition of Sample	21
1.3	Nationality of Responding Registrants	22
2.1	International Political Science Association, 1950–1985	33
2.2	Participation at IPSA World Congress, 1979	37
3.1	Variations in Professionalism and Internationalism	61
3.2	Intercorrelation of Scores on Scales	63
3.3	Perceived Value to Self of National, Regional, and Subdisciplinary Meetings	65
3.4	Chief Functions of International Scientific Congresses in Political Science	66
3.5	Registrants' Views on Functions of International Political Science Congresses	68
3.6	Importance of International Political Science Congresses	69
4.1	Expectations and Experiences: Mean Scores	80
4.2	Expectations, Experiences, and Professional Activity	83
4.3	Informal Contacts Established at IPSA World Congress, Moscow, 1979	89
4.4	Efforts to Keep Up with Colleagues Originally Met in Moscow	90

4.5	Impact of World Congresses on Participants' Scientific Work: A Comparison of Psychologists, Sociologists, and Political Scientists	92
4.6	Suggestions for Improving Future World Congresses: Views of Psychologists, Sociologists, and Political Scientists	95
5.1	Reasons Given for Attending or Not Attending the IPSA Moscow Meetings	105
5.2	Political Grounds for Evaluating IPSA's Decision on Moscow	108
5.3	Characteristics of Proponents and Opponents of Meetings in the USSR	109
5.4	Alternative Sites for IPSA World Congresses: Views of Registrants at the Moscow Meeting	111
5.5	Reasons Cited for Terming a Panel Session the Best or Worst	114
A.1	Breakdown of Registrants by Country	143
C.1	Professional Activity Scale	169
C.2	Professional Status Scale	170
C.3	International Research Competence Scale	171
C.4	International Activity Scale	172
C.5	IPSA Experience Scale	173

Figures

1.1	A Model of the Effects of an International Scientific Association	6

Preface

A peculiarity of human beings is that they carry through life a bundle of unexamined assumptions on the basis of which they act. Some of us do this more than others, of course, and there is always the possibility that, someday, one or another of us will look at what we are doing and ask why we are doing it and whether or not what we are doing will help us attain the goal toward which we are striving.

This is the case, we suggest, with respect to international scientific congresses (ISCs). We as scientists start with the assumption that effective science requires communication—an assumption that seems fair enough in its own right. Since many scientists are also teachers, and hence accustomed to verbal exchanges with students as well as colleagues, we quickly slip into the additional assumption that seminars and workshops are useful vehicles for scientific communication. If small meetings are good, then large meetings must be better since they bring together experts covering a wider range of topics. International conferences must be even better since they permit the expression of a still broader set of perspectives on the topics of interest to us. Ergo: International scientific congresses are vital to the advancement of science.

We assume other things about ISCs as well—that they are useful for transferring technologies (especially from developed to developing countries), that hosting them garners international respect for the sponsoring country, that attending them enhances the professional status of individual scientists and their institutions, and so forth. In a more general sense we sometimes assume that, by contributing to the international organization of science, ISCs facilitate the creation of world order and what Robert Angell (1969) called the "march toward peace."

But how do we know all this? Each individual who has attended an ISC doubtless returns home with some notion of how useful the particular meeting was in terms of learning something new, establishing contacts for possible future research, or simply visiting an interesting part of the world. We nevertheless have little generalized knowledge about the impact of ISCs on individual scientists, collective bodies (such as the international scientific associations that organize such meetings), a particular branch of science, or the establishment of world order. In short, we have never really examined our assumptions and tested them empirically.

Perhaps these unexamined assumptions are not overly problematic. If in doubt, we rhetorically ask ourselves no less than possible funding institutions, *why not* hold an international scientific congress? We *think* some good comes of them and, besides, they are not excessively expensive or difficult to organize.

There are several answers to such a rhetorical question, all seeking to balance the benefits of such congresses against their various kinds of costs. Without firm knowledge that ISCs are actually beneficial for advancing science, world order, or some general goal, we encounter severe difficulties in justifying their continuation in a world of scarce resources available for science.

For one thing, ISCs are indeed expensive in monetary terms. The budget of the 13th World Congress of the International Political Science Association (IPSA), held in July 1985 in Paris, was $150,000. Some 1,763 political scientists attended that meeting (not to speak of spouses, children, and others accompanying the participants). If we assume conservatively that the average participant spent $700 for transportation and $50 per day for six days for lodging and meals in Paris, paid $100 for IPSA membership and the congress registration fee, gave out $100 in incidental expenses, and devoted a week of salaried time to the meeting (at a rate of $20,800 per annum), then the real cost for that participant was approximately $1,600. Add to these sums approximately $150,000 for the direct costs of the program chairman and meetings of the international program committee, and we find that the total cost of the IPSA World Congress (deducting an amount for double-counting, but ignoring the association's general administrative expenses and the donated time of its officers) was in the neighborhood of $3 million—a major portion of it paid by governments, foundations, and universities in the form of individual travel grants.

Second, it is not clear that all scientists learn equally well from verbal interaction at large (or even small) conferences. If the question is the assimilation of new material, then the answer for many is clearly that an hour of reading refereed journals is more usefully spent than the same hour listening to someone making a formal presentation. If we broaden the question to more contextual factors, such as seeing how a productive scientist responds to challenges, or sharpening one's thinking skills by participating in the exchanges that follow the presentation of papers, or establishing contacts that may serve as the basis for future research, then we are in muddier waters. There is virtually no research on the actual effect of these activities, and none that we know of relating characteristics of conferences to individual styles of learning.

Third, can we comfortably believe that all, or some, or even a few ISCs contribute to the internationalization of science and that this, in turn, enhances world order? If we look at the political uses to which some international conferences have been put, then we might well respond negatively. Some writers have also feared what they term a "UNESCO-ization" of international scientific activity. By this they mean science run on the basis of "one nation, one vote," in which majority votes often based on political considerations can determine who is an acceptable invitee, what lines of inquiry are permissible, and which scientific results are to be credited.

It is important to obtain reliable data on such issues. If the benefits are low, especially in view of rising financial and perhaps political costs, then we may well want to consider new means of scientific communication to replace international scientific congresses (e.g., electronic mail). To continue unperturbed on an untenable path does not make good scientific (or fiscal) sense. Moreover, unless we have firm evidence that the benefits of ISCs significantly outweigh their costs in some general sense, then we as individual scientists who attend such congresses open ourselves to charges of academic profiteering—using the public purse for private gain.

This book reports on an effort to investigate systematically some of the uses and consequences of international scientific congresses. It seeks to improve the quality of scientific communication across national boundaries by examining the empirical basis of some of our assumptions. The procedure used in the study was to survey political scientists from nonsocialist countries who attended the 11th World Congress of the International Political Science Association (IPSA), held in August 1979 in Moscow, and also, by way of a control group, a random sample of political scientists from the United States and Canada who did not attend the Moscow meetings.

The assistance of several individuals and institutions enabled us to initiate and complete the project. Of particular importance was Judith Jones at the University of Illinois at Urbana-Champaign (UIUC), who coordinated all aspects of the project from the time we were considering the form of the questionnaires until the completed questionnaires were received and registered. Janie Carroll assisted during this period. Jutta Sebestik of the UIUC's Survey Research Laboratory helped us draft the questionnaires and resolve sampling problems. Barbara Hill, Department of Political Science at the University of Iowa, helped us develop the scales and process the data. Karl W. Deutsch of Harvard University and the Science Center Berlin, Jean A. Laponce of the University of British Columbia, Secretary General John E. Trent and former Executive Secretary Liette Boucher of the International Political Science

Association, Robert Alun Jones and Steven T. Seitz of UIUC, and Jerzy Wiatr of the University of Warsaw offered insightful comments that saved us from many an error. The UIUC's Research Board provided financial assistance at critical junctures. Anna J. Merritt of the Institute of Government and Public Affairs, UIUC, prepared the index. To all these individuals and institutions we are grateful.

Richard L. Merritt
Elizabeth C. Hanson

ONE

International Scientific Congresses: A Functional Approach

The world congress of an international scientific association is a peculiarly modern phenomenon. A Euro-American invention (Mead, 1968: 215), it brings together from all over the world scholars representing most aspects of a particular scientific discipline. It thus differs from a conference of experts on a single topic (see Capes, 1960) in the sense that the international scientific congress (ISC) presents a broad palette of sessions on a wide range of topics designed to appeal to both the specialist and the generalist, and to people with varying degrees of disciplinary sophistication.

Implicit in such a plan are several prerequisites. Some are physical and technical: conference facilities adequate for a large gathering, a staff trained in congress organization, inexpensive and convenient modes of transportation, and financial support from foundations, the participants' own universities, or elsewhere. Other prerequisites are structural and organizational. Among these are, most notably, a scientific discipline sufficiently developed that an international congress makes sense, an international scientific association representative of subdisciplinary concerns and the major countries where scientists identify themselves with the discipline, leadership capable of mounting such a congress, a communications network to facilitate the identification of topics of common interest, and the scientists who might have something important to say on them.

Perhaps the key prerequisite is a belief that an international scientific congress serves some function(s)—for the discipline, its members, or some other body.[1] But what are these functions? Or, more properly phrased, *who sees ISCs performing what functions, how, for whom, and with what effect?* It is this congeries of questions to which our study seeks at least partial answers.

The intuitively obvious answer to such a multifaceted question is that the world congress is an international communications medium to advance the state of science. That is, members of a scientific community (Polányi, 1951: 53-57; Shils, 1954) see the ISC as a means to learn more about the theories, findings, and methodologies in an area of scientific interest to them. Further reflection nevertheless reveals far greater complexity. Is the desire for scientific communication the sole motive underlying the individual scientist's decision to attend such a congress? If scientific communication is the goal, then is the ISC the most efficient or effective mechanism for achieving it? What interest do associational or governmental functionaries have in such congresses? Are there other functions so deeply embedded in the scientific enterprise that they all but escape the notice of casual or even experienced observers? As sociologists of science and scientific knowledge have shown us, easy answers to these questions do not lie at hand (Mulkay, 1979; Collins, 1983a, b; Jagtenberg, 1983).

And yet answers can be significant. They are germane to an emerging theory of science. As we shall see later, international scientific congresses play a role, implicitly or explicitly, in functional theories of international integration, structural theories of international relations (with their focus on center-periphery relations), and various approaches to the sociology and politics of science. If we would understand the nature of science and its relationship to society, then, information about the role played by ISCs can provide important clues.

On the more practical level of science policy, too, it makes sense to know what world congresses can and what they cannot accomplish. After all, an ISC is expensive in terms of time, money, and other resources, and hence constitutes a scientific investment. If its outcome in fact repays the investors by realizing their highest-priority goals, then they have sounder reasons to support future ISCs and perhaps even improve their financial and/or organizational foundation. If, however, world congresses do not accomplish what we intend them to, then we might think about restructuring them so that they will, or else consider alternative ways to meet these goals.

This chapter outlines a framework for analyzing the functionality of international scientific congresses. It looks first at the international scientific structure that has spawned ISCs in the first place. It then addresses the question of what individuals and other actors with stakes in a given scientific discipline consider the functions of ISCs to be. Finally, it describes a design for research aimed at answering some of the questions we have raised about the functionality of ISCs. The study explores such issues on the basis of a survey of political scientists from nonsocialist countries who attended (and some who did not attend) the 11th World Congress of the International Political Science Association, held in August 1979 in Moscow.

The Scientific Consociation

Our concern with science is, in fact, with some branch of science we may call a scientific discipline—chemistry, for instance, or physics or sociology.[2] Even so, the idea of a scientific discipline as such remains rather abstract. How can an observer identify, let us say, political science as a scientific discipline? What characterizes a scientific discipline best are, first, the distinctiveness of its subject matter and, second, the existence of a shared *myth* about its key dimensions. This myth, "the value-impregnated beliefs and notions that men hold, that they live by or live for" (MacIver, 1947: 4), lends integrative glue to a scientific discipline and sustains its activities.

"With the aid of authority," to follow MacIver's (1947: 42) line of reasoning, the "myth-conveyed scheme of values" determines the *order* of a scientific discipline.[3] What order myth backed by authority imposes on science has been the subject of intense dispute among theoreticians, and need not concern us here.[4] More to the point is the fact that various actors identify themselves with some version of the scientific order, make demands on it, and have certain expectations about its processes and outcomes, that is, they have *perspectives* on the scientific order (Lasswell and Kaplan, 1950: 25). Among these actors are not only producers of new knowledge but also those who organize facilities and raise funds to permit research to go on, see to the diffusion of knowledge throughout at least the discipline, apply it to practical problems, watch out for the interests of the scientists, and cover the financial and social costs of the particular scientific order. They are members of what we may call a disciplinary *scientific consociation*:[5]

1. Individual scientists who identify themselves with the scientific order of a given discipline, that is, generally accept its cognitive, normative, and behavioral standards, conduct research within its framework, and transmit these perspectives to their students

2. Research organizations—universities, government laboratories, research institutes in the private sector, or other—in which the scientists work, and which set priorities for their research

3. Disciplinary associations at various levels (local or regional, national, international), which seek to play an authoritative role in interpreting the myth of the scientific order, safeguarding standards, distributing rewards, and otherwise promoting the interests of the discipline itself as well as associational members[6]

4. National governments, which represent the societies that ultimately pay for science and expect it to be useful

To these some would add a fifth relevant actor:

5. Global society, to which writers have attributed functional needs

(ranging from hyperstability to a full-scale redistribution of resources) that science could, in their view, help meet

Each of these actors has a stake in the development of a scientific discipline; and, we would argue, a part of their perspectives on that discipline and its scientific order focuses on the functionality of international scientific congresses.

Regrettably, however, we do not know much about the place of ISCs in the diverse actors' perspectives. Some elements of this puzzle we may infer from empirically based research on other matters—the fact, for instance, that perspectives vary from one actor to the next. Variation occurs both within a single level of actor and across levels. Thus two scientists may have significantly different constellations of identifications, demands, and expectations; and the way in which those responsible for a research organization define research priorities may clash with the views of scientists who must conduct the research. It follows that behavior based on these perspectives, including developing such mechanisms as world congresses, may be mutually incompatible for those with an interest in the outcome. All this is a way of saying that what is functional for one actor may be dysfunctional for another, especially in a setting of competition for scarce resources.

For the rest, the research literature is curiously spotty. It has devoted considerable attention to some aspects of the structures that "represent" scientific disciplines—descriptive histories of national scientific associations, the operation and impact of scientific journals, and disciplinary reward structures—while leaving others virtually untouched. This is true with respect to disciplinary congresses at whatever level, and also with respect to international disciplinary associations as such. Brief attention to the latter may serve as an introduction to the problématique of their congresses.

Growth of International Science

The emergence of an organizational framework for international science has been an integral part of an even broader trend. The 20th century, particularly the era since 1945, has witnessed a dramatic increase in both the number of international nongovernmental organizations (INGOs)—organizations of private groups and individuals that share common interests across national boundaries—and the scope of their activities. Not surprisingly, this trend has stimulated considerable scholarly interest in the role that these nonstate actors play in an international system dominated by nation-states. Numbering less than 200 in 1909, they increased by mid-century to approximately 1,000 and by 1984 to 4,615 (Union of Intergovernmental Associations, 1984: i,1626).

International scientific and professional associations constitute nearly half the total number of INGOs. International *scientific* associations contribute to a growing body of knowledge and technology by aiding the communication of scientific findings, stimulating new research, improving methods of analysis, and facilitating international collaboration in research. International *professional* associations, serving the public with a body of applied systematic knowledge, seek to maintain high levels of competence and ethical standards. Our focus is the former, international scientific associations. Of particular interest to analysts have been the ways in which and extent to which these prolific transnational phenomena influence international policies and the political and social consequences of their activities in the aggregate.

From one point of view, international scientific associations are simply a means to pursue individual and group interests at the international level (Crane, 1981). They act as pressure groups exerting influence on intergovernmental organizations and governments to adopt certain policies. Establishing an international association with a permanent secretariat and procedures for periodic meetings helps national associations and individual members in various parts of the world to communicate, coordinate their activities, and cooperate for the purpose of furthering the goals of the discipline. Transnational activities can give status and visibility to the associations and individuals that pursue them. They can stimulate the growth and expansion of a discipline or profession by such means as encouraging the establishment of new national associations, curricula, research institutes, and training programs. Figure 1.1 presents William M. Evan's (1975) neat summary of an international scientific association's various activities and effects. More generally, the eminent French political scientist and first secretary general of the International Political Science Association, Jean Meynaud (1961: 12), concluded that, "in the tremendous and indispensable effort to convert the present-day world to the social sciences," international social scientific associations "played a very honourable part."

From another point of view, through their activities some of these associations have sought to influence international decisionmaking and the international system as a whole. Curtis Roosevelt (1970), for example, saw an important role for various types of nongovernmental organizations in the development of "constituencies" that can mobilize public opinion and support for world development goals. Several articles in the published proceedings of a conference on international scientific and professional associations (Evan, 1981a) emphasized their potential role in promoting the growth of transnational values and in advancing peace and justice. According to this view, these associations increase the level of integration among nation-states by multiplying international contacts and by creating a network of relationships that socialize members into the values of transnationalism. In his introduction the volume's editor (Evan, 1981b: 16, 23) argued that the

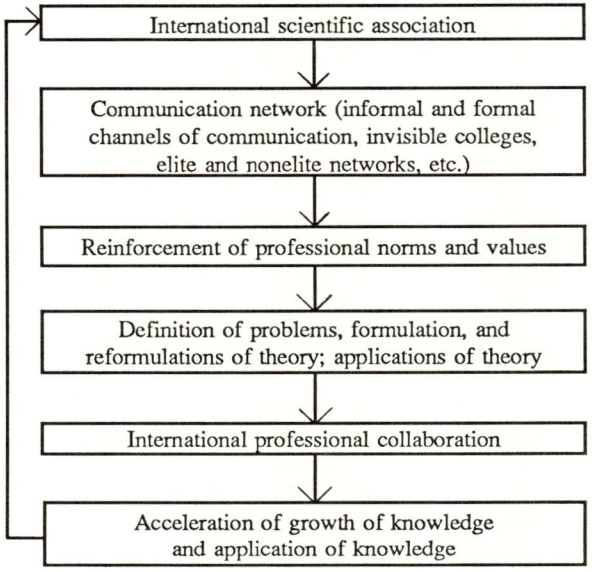

Source: Evan, 1975: 386.

Figure 1.1 A Model of the Effects of an International Scientific Association

activities of international scientific and professional associations reinforce the ethos of science and the commitment of scientists to the cultural values of universalism, communality, disinterestedness, and organized skepticism. If any segment of society can help the international system to move "from nationalist values to transnational humanist values," he concluded, it is the international community of scientists, engineers, and other professionals.

Louis Kriesberg (1981) suggested how the activities of international scientific and professional associations directly and indirectly contribute to the attainment of justice and the reduction of violence. One way is by providing a source of ideas for mutually acceptable solutions to intergovernmental problems and a setting in which new insights emerge from the discussions among private individuals from different countries. They can also provide less advantaged members with services and benefits aimed at helping them to solve their problems and advance their knowledge and skills. In the long term Kriesberg anticipated that these associations will aid the development of a common world culture by increasing awareness and tolerance of differences; and, as an extreme possibility, they may strengthen alternative transnational structures by providing quasi-governmental services.

A more ambivalent viewpoint emerged from a seminar, on "Social Science as a Transnational System," in which 15 social scientists from various regions of the world participated. The summary of the discussions (Alger and Lyons, 1974) emphasized the need for a global community of social scientists responsive to the growing number of global problems and the value of transnational activities for generating, disseminating, and applying social science knowledge. At the same time, some participants expressed concern that increased international cooperation in the social sciences under the present conditions will only strengthen existing patterns of dependency. International scientific associations, they pointed out, play an important role in establishing and maintaining contacts and communication among social scientists from the dominant centers; but in performing this role they tend to institutionalize the dependency relations of social scientists outside the dominant centers. Some empirical evidence of this tendency appeared in Kjell Skjelsbaek's (1971) analysis of INGOs. Citing the high density of INGO comemberships among the developed countries and the lower level of participation in these organizations by the less developed countries, he suggested that INGOs can lead to a higher degree of integration among the countries that are already dominant and thus help consolidate and enhance their position.

A main task of international scientific associations, however they are viewed, is to organize and convene international congresses and other meetings. These occasions as a rule involve more members than any other single activity of a given association, and they provide one of the most important mechanisms for conducting the association's work and implementing its goals. Hundreds of international scientific congresses occur every year, covering subjects from thermodynamics to the training of midwives. Table 1.1 shows that the number of international meetings for both nongovernmental and intergovernmental organizations increased between 1950 and 1983 by almost 6 percent annually. Although the international meetings of intergovernmental organizations (IGOs) are more frequent, those of INGOs involve more participants. For example, in 1978 only 250,000 people attended the 5,000 meetings organized by IGOs,[7] whereas 2 million participated in the 4,800 meetings sponsored by INGOs (Fighiera, 1984: 143).

Accompanying this growth in the number of international meetings has been their expansion to include an ever larger number and ever wider variety of countries. The geographical distribution of meetings shown in Table 1.1 indicates this development. The overwhelming majority of these meetings in the last two decades took place in Western Europe. As far as international scientific associations are concerned, a discrepancy has existed between the location of most scholars (North America) and the location of most

Table 1.1 Growth and Geographical Distribution of International Meetings, 1950-1983[a]
(Intergovernmental and Nongovernmental Organizations)

Region	1950 No.	1950 %	1955 No.	1955 %	1960 No.	1960 %	1965 No.	1965 %	1970 No.	1970 %	1975 No.	1975 %	1980 No.	1980 %	1983 No.	1983 %
Western Europe	578	80	843	75	1257	66	1115	63	850	63	1887	57	2915	61	2851	59
North America	70	10	85	8	160	8	193	11	133	10	441	14	633	13	691	14
Latin America	36	5	81	7	181	9	120	7	85	6	203	6	183	4	189	4
Asia/Pacific	23	3	66	5	143	8	166	9	152	11	376	11	590	12	668	14
Eastern Europe	8	1	22	2	87	5	111	6	104	8	276	8	339	7	296	6
Africa	9	1	28	2	71	4	63	3	29	2	137	4	152	3	169	3
Total	724	100	1125	100	1899	100	1768	100	1353	100	3320	100	4812	100	4864	100

[a]Meetings organized and/or sponsored by international associations listed in Union of International Associations (1983). Percentages may not add up to 100 because of rounding.

Sources: Union of International Associations Bulletin NGO, 4,2 (February 1952): 64-65; Union of International Associations Monthly Review, 8,4 (April 1966): 207-209; International Associations, 20,2 (February 1968): 92-95; International Transnational Associations, 24,1 (January 1972): 47-49; ibid., 29,1-2 (January-February 1977): 43-45; ibid., 34,1 (January-February 1982): 42-43; and ibid., 37,1 (January-February 1985): 58-59. Fighiera (1984: 145) has slightly different figures.

congresses (Western Europe). A simple explanation is the fact that international-minded people want to meet "abroad." Accordingly, the more North Americans there are in these associations, the less they want to meet in North America. It is also true that, by and large, North Americans have enjoyed greater access to travel funds. This lopsidedness is nevertheless changing. Other regions have shared in the general increase in numbers of international meetings. The proportion of meetings held in Western Europe has, in fact, declined substantially from 80 percent in 1950 to 59 percent in 1983. In part this reflects growth in the scientific establishments of other countries, in part a growing demand by these countries for scientific recognition. The result of these trends is that more non-European countries have had an opportunity to host an international meeting, and more of their nationals have been able to attend.

Functions of International Scientific Congresses

The periodic international congress has become a focal point of activity for most international scientific associations. It is typically a very large meeting which covers a wide range of topics and is attended by a geographically diverse group of participants. Although the subject matter varies from one discipline to another, certain practices and procedures have become common features. Advance planning, a not unproblematic logistical task, is carried out by the multinational executive and program committees together with the association's secretariat. These plans include decisions about the site and physical arrangements as well as the agenda, procedures, and participants.

The day for the congress arrives. Typically, an opening ceremony, sometimes including a welcoming address from a high political official of the host country, eases the participants into the theme and procedures of the congress and, afterwards, may provide an occasion for informal interaction. Participants must then choose for the rest of the week among a smorgasbord of smaller sessions, usually panels in which a particular topic is addressed from several points of view. In such panels, participants summarize orally the theoretical analyses and research results contained in their papers, which they have made available for distribution, and a brief discussion follows, sometimes led by designated commentators. Alternatively, roundtables eschew the formal presentation and critique of papers in favor of maximizing informal exchanges among the panelists. Additional discussion typically ensues in the corridors and more pleasant places. A grand reception and/or banquet and sometimes other events further facilitate informal interaction. The congress ends as it began, in a plenary session at which all relevant persons are thanked and the significance of the congress reaffirmed.

Just what international scientific congresses accomplish remains an open question. A considerable body of literature on intergovernmental conferences notwithstanding, little scholarly attention has been given to the international meetings of nongovernmental organizations in general or to those of international scientific associations in particular.[8] The gap in the literature is remarkable in view of the growth of this kind of transnational activity and the vast amount of human and financial resources that planning, conducting, and participating in these congresses absorb.

Given what participants and observers have written about the functionality of international scientific congresses, what is it we think we know? And what else do we want to find out? The following sections address these questions by focusing in turn on each of the five categories of actors identified earlier as having an interest in international scientific congresses: individual scientists, research organizations, disciplinary associations, national governments (representing their societies), and global society.

Individual Scientists

A relatively small portion of the membership of the relevant discipline actually attends a given international scientific congress. Why is this? One response is certainly that constraints of time, cost, convenience, and still other technical factors conspire to keep people away. If we assume, however, that these constraints are fairly constant across the membership of the discipline in any single country, we are left with a slightly modified version of our question. Why do some scientists in a country—or at a single university—choose to attend an ISC while their colleagues do not?

Personal characteristics. We might seek the answer to this question in terms of sociological differences that characterize scientists. Thus a comprehensive survey of the American professoriat by Everett Carll Ladd, Jr. and Seymour Martin Lipset (1978) confirmed widespread assumptions about the existence of an "academic jet set" elite and suggested certain hypotheses about its members. Of the faculty members they surveyed, 79 percent had never attended an international scientific meeting abroad; only 2 percent had traveled abroad for this purpose 10 or more times. These "high travelers" came overwhelmingly from major research universities, were heavily involved in research, and in the course of their careers most had published at least 20 professional articles.

Another answer lies in scientists' perceptions of what they might derive from attending such congresses. Even if an individual has been invited to present a paper at an ISC, expects to be free when it takes place, and has the requisite funding, the decision to accept the invitation entails an opportunity cost. The time, money, and energy that would be required could be spent in other ways. Assuming rationality, the individual must weigh the costs against the particular congress's functionality for meeting certain scientific, professional, and personal goals.

Scientific communication. We noted earlier the most commonly heard assumption about ISCs, that they are an important means of scientific communication. Thus the 13th report of the National Science Board to Congress on the status of science and technology in the United States asserts that international scientific congresses provide a faster method of communicating research results than publication, as well as immediate feedback and ideas from colleagues. The informal exchange of ideas, the report continues, can lead to "modifications of research, collaborative efforts, and elimination of duplicate work" (National Science Board, 1981: 41).

The extent to which international scientific congresses in fact advance scientific knowledge, however, has rarely been investigated scientifically. The most notable effort came from the Center for Research in Scientific Communication of Johns Hopkins University, which surveyed delegates to the International Congress of Psychology, held in 1966 in Moscow, and the World Congress of Sociology held in the same year in Evian, France. These studies sought to ascertain the information effects of an international congress by analyzing the scientific information exchange and interaction that resulted from these two meetings. The project's final report (Johns Hopkins University, 1968: 64) concluded among other things that:

> The research scientist today feels strongly that he should be free to disseminate his results to an international audience, to receive publications from and establish information exchange with colleagues in laboratories throughout the world, and to have personal interaction with experts in his field, regardless of the country in which an expert is located. The two international meetings studied to some extent facilitated each of these pursuits. . . . In the present day state of science, with scientific information accumulating in great quantity, the individual scientist relies on an international meeting every two or three years to bring himself up to date on new international developments in his field and to revitalize his international information-exchange network.

A closer examination of the project's data, as we shall see in Chapter 4, nonetheless reveals that these effects were far from universal among the participating psychologists and sociologists and far from uniform even among those reporting them.

Professional advancement. As long as opportunities to participate in an ISC are scarce, scientists will view them as part of their reward structure. For some it provides immediate gratification in the form of status vis-à-vis departmental and other colleagues who were not invited or could not raise the necessary funds. The act of presenting one's research before a panel of other scientists, distinguished at least by the fact that they, too, were invited to attend the congress, may also enhance one's professional reputation.

Doubtless more enduring is the recognition that one's research is sufficiently important to merit an international hearing. On the one hand, this recognition may make it more possible for the scientist to secure grants, publication outlets, professional offices, invitations to further congresses, and other preferments. On the other hand, it gains a potentially significant audience for the research itself. This may encourage scientists elsewhere to take the approach and findings more seriously, which in turn lends legitimacy to the particular research enterprise.

International scientific congresses also offer opportunities to the scientist interested in taking an active role in shaping the profession. They are an excellent occasion for learning about the association's power structure and who is who in it. Contacts with key individuals may in turn lead to appointments to the program or other committees, in which organizational decisions are made about the content of future conferences, structure of the association's publication activities, and the distribution of its rewards.

Personal enrichment. It is difficult to ignore the fact that the scientist who attends a meeting overseas gains something beyond scientific and professional growth. Other advantages include having opportunities for travel and recreation, enjoying the conviviality of shared experiences with old and new friends, sampling exotic foods, and enhancing one's status among friends and neighbors. Cynics have asserted that these benefits are indeed the primary factor moving scholars to seek to attend international meetings, and that any scientific reason volunteered by participants is more a justificatory ruse than an accurate assessment of their true motives. It follows, in this view, that the professional prestige gained has as its most important value attracting invitations to yet other such meetings. In his satire describing the "small world" and multifarious escapades of scholarly jet-setters attending international conferences, the English novelist David Lodge (1984: 238) wryly noted: "Afterwards, when they are back home, and friends and family ask if they enjoyed the conference, they say, oh yes, but not so much for the papers, which were pretty boring, as for the informal contacts one makes on those occasions."

We must not be too hasty in writing off such motives as frivolous. To be sure, given the scarcity of opportunities to attend ISCs, doubtless few foundations or universities will wish to support the participant who appears to be seeking pleasure alone. For the others, however, the ego gratification derived from presenting a paper, travel, and the like may have a strong scientific value as well. A Dutch "founding father" of the International

Political Science Association expressed this possibility well. The organization of international congresses, he wrote (Barents, 1959: 1090),

> by the ingenious systems of travel subsidies which accompany most of them, acts as an inexpensive travel agency for relatively poor people like university teachers. This is not a cynical comment. To some people regular visits to international congresses have an aspect of profiteering, but for many scholars, particularly of the younger generation, it would be quite impossible to travel all over the world without outside financial help. Travelling, if wisely done, being part of one's education, this function of international congresses may be something to be regarded with a watchful eye, but is in itself to be neither despised nor neglected.

The chance to stand up in front of an audience of peers to deliver a paper may similarly accomplish more than merely massaging the ego. As suggested earlier, and as the study of the world congresses of psychologists and sociologists showed (Johns Hopkins University, 1968: 64):

> Making a presentation placed an author in the "limelight" and attracted other workers in the field to him for discussion of areas of mutual interest. Information exchange as a result of having made a presentation at these meetings was frequent, had important effects on authors' work, and served as a stimulus for the establishment of continuing personal information exchange and, consequently, of the development or extension of informal, international communication networks.

And it may very well be that "the informal contacts one makes on those occasions" provide important new insights and the basis for innovative research.

Research Organizations

Universities, research institutes, and other agencies stand to benefit when their staff members participate in international scientific congresses, especially, of course, if these individuals are highly visible or successful in their activities. First, the participants may return from an ISC with enhanced knowledge, skills, and self-confidence that improve their productivity and hence augment their value to their home research organizations. Second, the participant, when presenting theories and findings, in a sense "represents" the research organization. The presentation tells other scientists what kind of work the organization deems significant as well as the quality of researcher it employs. A successful paper by one of its scientists may enhance the international credibility of the organization as a whole. Third, the organization whose scientists participate regularly in ISCs and whose projects gain an international audience may be able to retail such recognition in the form of greater attractiveness for potential recruits and improved access to research funds.

Disciplinary Associations

International scientific congresses may serve several functions for *national scientific associations* and their regional and subdisciplinary components.[9] For one thing, despite assertions that science has been internationalized, a residue of national competitiveness persists in many disciplines.[10] Certainly, scientific productivity and training facilities play the major role in assessing claims to precedence, but the number and quality of scientists national associations send to international meetings are also important. To the extent that the research frameworks of these scientists dominate the intellectual interaction, their national associations can be said to dominate the discipline.

Also, a national association seeking to gain greater prestige and enhance its role in the international association may try especially hard to send many of its members to the congress. Such behavior may be instrumental in obtaining yet another goal: a more important role in the international association itself. A greater presence at the congress may improve the likelihood that the national association's candidates will be selected to serve as officers of the association, its ideas given greater weight in organizing the succeeding congress, or its offer to host future meetings taken more seriously. At the same time, however, implicit in this process is occasionally the desire to control access to the international congress on the part of the country's scientists. While some national associations are content to let the international association's program committee determine whom to invite, others want to exercise a veto to ensure that the "right kind" of national scientists attend (for example, only those who are members of the national association or who toe a particular ideological or paradigmatic line). Especially important in this respect is the national association's ability to determine who receives travel grants or, in some countries, permission to travel abroad.

The national association that hosts an international congress may profit in several ways. The most obvious of these are, first, an enriched national discipline because of its improved opportunities for scientific communication, which in turn may strengthen the national association; and, second, the national association's greater visibility or prestige in the international disciplinary setting. It also certifies to its government the national association's relative importance in that setting. This in turn may have implications for future financial or other support for the association. A fourth outcome may be that the national association gains greater influence over the content of the congress. Although, to be sure, an international program committee usually determines what will be discussed, it is unlikely to ignore the favorite themes of the host association. Finally, hosting an international congress gives the national association opportunities to increase its sway over the members of the discipline in its own country. That is, it becomes quite visible as the national discipline's chief organizing force, in control of important resources such as access to the international communications network.

For the *international scientific association*, the congress it organizes also serves multiple purposes. Some of these meet general disciplinary needs: advancing the state of knowledge in the discipline, developing a sense of scientific community among its members, and focusing on the discipline international attention, albeit modest and fleeting. Then, too, a congress responds to some of the international association's structural needs. The fact that national associations and scientists from all over the world heed its call to convene is an important legitimation of the international association's existence and *raison d'être*. Its organization of the congress, through such organs as its secretariat and program committee, facilitates the association's control over the structure of the discipline as a whole, besides giving it greater standing in the international community of scientific disciplines. Moreover, we should not forget that association officers obtain their own rewards from a successful congress.

International scientific associations face an important strategic question that can affect the functionality of ISCs for them. Most scientific disciplines are moving toward a fragmentation of knowledge, in which specialists focus on ever smaller areas of research. An effect can be that the association becomes a holding company for a number of subdisciplinary interest groups. In such circumstances, how should the association organize its congresses? One answer points toward associational centralism. It embodies a "top-down" approach, in which an authoritative program committee identifies what it considers to be the discipline's core topics and integrates papers linked to these topics. Another answer stresses disciplinary pluralism—a "bottom-up" approach that envisions a broad palette of more specific research topics that may or may not fit well together. If it is true that the one approach runs the danger of promoting a sterile "official science," then it is also the case that the other could easily undermine the discipline's intellectual coherence. Steering a course between the two shoals, albeit far from simple, is necessary since either could make the association virtually irrelevant to its members, that is, deinstitutionalize it.

National Governments

Normally, a country benefits in numerous small ways from hosting an international scientific congress. Bringing to one of its cities several hundred or a few thousand foreigners has an impact on the country's tourist industry.

For a country short of foreign exchange, this can be a powerful incentive to encourage such congresses. The fact that many of these foreigners are first-rate scientists may improve the quality of the country's own scientific establishment. Not only will the participants exchange scientific information that may be of value to indigenous scientists and academic administrators, but their mere presence may inspire one's own scientists to greater achievements. A strengthened national scientific establishment in turn contributes to the country's international power capabilities.[11]

Such a conclave of distinguished scientists may yield other benefits as well: prestige for the country's scientific establishment and the government that supports it, an enhanced reputation as a place in which free scientific exchanges can take place, greater understanding on the participants' part of the country's political and other problems, and perhaps even more warmth toward the country itself and its inhabitants. All these in turn may serve the political interests of the government, indeed so much so that some governments may be tempted to manipulate the congress to produce the greatest possible political gains.

Normally, too, ISCs entail some costs for the host country. Its government usually must make available, or encourage its private foundations to provide, a substantial sum to facilitate the congress's organization. In the national budgets of most countries, the amount of money needed is usually trivial (however difficult it may be for congress organizers to extract it!). Another cost is the risk that the congress will be less than successful, and leave in the participants' mouths a bad taste toward the country as a whole. Some countries even fear that conferees may criticize the government (see Dickson, 1979) or else envision possible problems ensuing from too much interaction between foreign scientists and the local citizenry. They may thus refuse permission to a scientific body seeking to organize a congress on their soil or, if they grant it, impose restrictions on the press or isolate the congress itself in some idyllic spot far distant from potentially troublesome population centers.

The importance of international scientific congresses in the eyes of national governments makes them a legitimate object in interstate struggles. At one level governments can treat ISCs in an avowedly political fashion. Thus, the government of state X might declare that its national scientific associations should ensure that world congresses are not held in opposing state Y, or that it will refuse permission for its scientists to attend congresses in Y. Such open boycotts are known in sports as well as science. At another level, the scientific establishment of country X, with or without the backing of its government, may seek to influence country Y's behavior. It might declare that its members should not attend congresses in or otherwise cooperate with scientists in country Y because of some action by the latter's government (such as perceived violations of the "human rights" of scientists or others)—and then apply heavy pressure on individual scientists in X (and perhaps elsewhere) to comply with the injunction (Seltzer, 1978; Stone and Spilhaus, 1980).

Global Society

Insofar as holding or boycotting international scientific congresses has an impact on a nation-state's power capabilities, such actions pertain to the broader realm of international relations. They fit, first of all, into *systemic theories of international relations*, which posit alternative structures of the international system and the modes of interaction appropriate to each. A balance-of-power system, stressing flexible behavior among states that cooperate and confront as a balancing mechanism, is doubtless less likely to intermix politics and science than is a rigid bipolar system characterized by opposed ideologies or ways of life. Similarly, a state trying to ease relations with another may see scientific exchanges, including joint conferences and cooperation at international congresses, as a first step.

The latter possibility has led not a few writers to see an important role for science in their *functional theories of international political integration*. World congresses, this argument runs, help to internationalize science, and internationalized science can contribute to world order and peace. Referring specifically to international professional and scientific associations, Robert C. Angell (1981: 244) argued that "the very existence of a global association strengthens existing ties across national boundaries and inaugurates new ones." The consequence is not only improved scientific communication or expansion of professional norms. Rather, the elaboration of such webs of interaction invites a government to benefit from their existence and puts it on notice that political action to tear them apart entails at least some costs in terms of lost benefits. Angell thus concludes that such associations "have become working elements in the world institutional structure that is slowly fostering intersocietal and intercultural integration" (p. 254). More generally, "transnational participation," of which these associations are one form, "will gradually carry the world over the threshold of peace" (Angell, 1969: 28).

It is of course possible to make a contrary argument. A poorly conceived or implemented world congress may make national associations wonder about the utility of continuing to pay their annual assessments to the international scientific association, and sour individual scientists on the whole idea of such an association for their discipline. The attempt by a host country to use a congress for its own political purposes may create enough hostility to split the association. Or the congress organizers, by choosing papergivers according to criteria of geographic representativeness to the exclusion of considerations of quality, may trivialize the association for important segments of its membership. Any of these occurrences could hamper rather than enhance the prospects for international cooperation at the scientific and even political level.

Some recent *theories on structure and change in the global system* offer contradictory notions about the role of science and international scientific congresses. More benign approaches see in them opportunities for developed countries to transfer technologies to the less developed (Hanson and Merritt, 1983). Some conferences are specifically geared to this end. Thus the American Chemical Society workshop held in Cairo in 1977 focused on publicly available technology in five chemical subject areas that constituted serious economic problems for Egypt. In other, more general congresses, too, participation by its scholars can indirectly augment a country's level of technological know-how. The perceived effect in either case is progress toward reducing the gap between the world's rich and poor.

More critical analyses of North-South relations (see Alger and Lyons, 1974) have highlighted a different pattern. Historically, in this view, (North-)Western scientists have dominated the international associations and their paradigms the scientific literature. These scientists have in effect forced on emergent science in the Third World their own paradigms, irrespective of whether or not these paradigms are appropriate; and their control of the major journals makes it difficult for scientists with alternative paradigms to secure a hearing. An international scientific congress, by emphasizing research paradigms that are predominantly Western, thus fosters "dependency" on the part of Third World states. Acting as professional "gatekeepers" (see Becker and Horowitz, 1972; Broadhead and Rist, 1976), congress organizers select among Third World applicants those whose work has adopted or is at least compatible with these paradigms. If this is true, then the congress is not truly addressing the needs of the less developed countries but is deepening the gap between them and the industrialized West and ensuring the latter's dominance over the former.

Functional Equivalents

As we look at the multiplicity of functions ostensibly served by ISCs for various members of a scientific consociation, it is useful to bear in mind the possibility that some of them have functional equivalents. That is, some other structure or process may meet the needs of an institution, organization, or society just as well as an ISC does. We might argue that, if an ISC's sole function is the communication of formal scientific knowledge, then journals can accomplish the same function more effectively and less expensively (Menzel, 1959). Alternatively, if we justify ISCs solely in terms of informal communication taking place among experts in a given field, then we might consider whether "invisible colleges" are more efficacious in serving this function (Price, 1961: 99; Crane, 1972). But, if formal and informal scientific communication takes its place alongside serendipitous learning, expanding the network in a particular line of research, and still other uses, and if we consider several of these functions vital, then no exact functional equivalent to an ISC may exist from the vantage point of the individual scientist.

Perceptions and Realities: A Design for Research

The many actors constituting a scientific consociation—individual scientists, research organizations, disciplinary associations at various levels, national governments, and global society—thus all have reasons to support (or, in some cases, disparage) the idea of holding international scientific congresses. Whether or not these diverse actors recognize such reasons as valid functions of ISCs is quite another question, one for empirical research. Ideally, such a research project would interview individuals representing all the actors to secure their perspectives, and examine behaviors and other evidence to ascertain the extent to which the reported perceptions match developments in the real world of science.

The research reported in this volume makes a beginning toward understanding the functionality of international scientific congresses by surveying the perceptions of individual scientists. A year after the event we sent printed questionnaires to participants (and nonparticipants) in the 11th World Congress of the International Political Science Association (IPSA), held in August 1979 in Moscow. Such a procedure raises a fundamental question: How do we interpret the results? Assuming (as we do) that respondents accurately recorded their views, what will their comments tell us? How well do these views mirror those of actors other than themselves? After all, individual scientists are seldom in a position to assess directly an ISC's functionality for a disciplinary association or government, not to mention an inchoate global society.

The simple answer is that the respondents' perceptions of this functionality form a reality for them. This assertion has three implications for our research. First, their personal "reality" is what leads scientists to decide whether or not to attend an ISC. Because in a very real sense ISCs are meaningless without the participation of an international array of scientists, the aggregate of individual realities is crucial to an ISC's success or failure. Second, we must pay close attention to what individual scientists see to be functional and what they fail to recognize as such. Are the imputed functions in the latter category simply irrelevant, better performed by functional equivalents to the ISC, or vital but not especially noticeable by the individual (latent functions)? The answer to this kind of question is important for those who organize and fund ISCs as well as to theorists of international science. Third, our evaluation of perceived functionalities for actors other than individual scientists must rely heavily on inferences drawn from the recorded responses and ancillary information.

Sample

To explore the impact of the Moscow meetings we sent separate questionnaires to two samples: registrants, or political scientists (and others) from nonsocialist countries who registered to attend these meetings; and nonregistrants, a control group randomly selected from the political science profession in the United States and Canada, but excluding any persons on the first list.

Registrants. In accordance with prior agreements among the congress's organizers, all participants from countries outside the ruble currency area were supposed to pre-register at IPSA's secretariat in Ottawa, Canada. Payment of a registration fee of $75 for professionals or $25 for students entitled the registrant to both an official invitation to the congress and the certification of registration necessary for obtaining a Soviet visa, as well as to materials provided at the congress itself. Participants from the ruble currency area were to pre-register or register with the Soviet organizing committee. We decided to limit our survey to scholars who pre-registered in Ottawa. Of the 1,027 registrants to whom we sent questionnaires, 420 (41%) completed and returned them (Table 1.2).

The list of registrants provided by IPSA's secretariat is not identical with the list of those from the nonsocialist world who actually attended the meetings in Moscow.[12] First, some who registered ultimately found it impossible to make the trip, for financial, time, health or other reasons. To the best of the organizers' knowledge, no one remained home because Soviet authorities denied them visas—although in some cases problems associated with obtaining visas led people to decide against going to Moscow. Of the 420 registrants responding to our questionnaire, 15 (3%) reported that they did not attend the congress and another did not indicate whether he attended or not.

Second, a few individuals, especially those such as Herbert Aptheker of the United States who were invited directly by the Soviet organizers, made their own arrangements with the latter's office in Moscow and hence do not appear on the registration lists prepared in Ottawa. Third, in one of those vagaries of international tourism, a group of perhaps a hundred Mexicans discovered that joining IPSA and paying the registration fee enabled them to take an unusually inexpensive guided tour of the Soviet Union; none, however, seems to have attended any IPSA function in Moscow or to have

Table 1.2 Size and Composition of Sample

Region	Number of Questionnaires Sent	Number of Questionnaires Returned	Percentage Returned
A. Registrants			
North America	305	217	71%
United States	(249)	(180)	(72)
Canada	(56)	(37)	(66)
Other West (incl. Israel)	432	157	36
Third World[a]	290	46	16
Total	1027	420	41%
B. Nonregistrants			
United States	428	214	50%
APSA members	(324)	(163)	(50)
Graduate dep'ts	(104)	(51)	(49)
Canada (CPSA members)	62	24	39
Total	490	238	49%

[a]Includes questionnaires sent to but not returned by approximately 100 tourists who registered for the IPSA meetings but did not attend; if the number of questionnaires sent is reduced by this figure (or if we take IPSA's official tally of 194 actual participants from the Third World), then the percentage-returned figure rises to 24 percent for the Third World and 45 percent for the entire sample.

filled out and returned our questionnaire. Table 1.3 shows the national origin of the 420 responding registrants (see Appendix A for details).

Nonregistrants. To ascertain the extent to which registrants at the IPSA congress were representative of the larger population of political scientists, we developed a second sample of professional political scientists in North America who did not register to attend the Moscow meetings. Anticipating a lower rate of response from these nonregistrants, we deliberately oversampled to ensure that the number of returned questionnaires from registrants and nonregistrants would be roughly equal. The sample was drawn from three sources. First, we selected from the *American Political Science Association Membership Directory, 1980* every 28th name with an address in the United States. Second, taking into account the fact that at least half of the country's professional political scientists are not members of APSA, and our observation that APSA's membership roster includes a large

Table 1.3 Nationality of Responding Registrants
(as indicated by place of work)

Country	No.	Country	No.
North America		Latin America	
United States	180	Mexico	8
Canada	37	Brazil	3
	217	Chile	1
			12
Other Western			
Germany (FRG)	26	Africa and Middle East	
Sweden	21	Turkey	7
United Kingdom	20	Ivory Coast	1
Netherlands	18	Nigeria	1
Norway	13		9
Denmark	10		
Finland	10	Asia and Pacific	
France	8	Japan	10
Israel	7	India	7
Spain	6	South Korea	4
Switzerland	6	Hong Kong	1
Australia	3	Malaysia	1
Greece	3	Philippines	1
Italy	3	Singapore	1
Belgium	2		25
Ireland	1		
	157	Total Third World	46

Total respondents = 420

number of graduate students, few of whom seemed likely to be knowledgeable about international conferences, we sent a questionnaire to every 45th faculty member listed in the APSA's *Guide to Graduate Study in Political Science, 1980*. Third, we sampled every fifth name from a membership list provided by the Canadian Political Science Association (CPSA). In each case we skipped over persons who had registered to attend the IPSA meetings in Moscow. Of the 490 nonregistrants to whom we sent questionnaires, 238 (49%) completed and returned them (Table 1.2).

Questionnaires

We designed the questionnaires after extensive consultation with North American colleagues who had attended the IPSA meetings in Moscow and with the expert advice of Jutta Sebestik of the Survey Research Laboratory, University of Illinois at Urbana-Champaign; we revised them after some pretesting among professional colleagues. The 15-page questionnaire for registrants includes both open- and closed-ended questions which, we anticipated, would require approximately an hour to complete conscientiously. The eight-page questionnaire for nonregistrants contains (mostly closed-ended) questions taken from the questionnaire for registrants, and was designed to be completed in about 15 minutes. (See Appendix B for the questionnaires.)

The questionnaires include four kinds of questions. The first category sought to obtain biographical information about the respondents: professional background and status, attendance at national and international conferences, skill in foreign languages, and the like. Another set of questions aimed at eliciting in open-ended fashion opinions about the functions served by national professional meetings as well as international scientific conferences. A third set focused specifically on the issue of site selection—especially Moscow as the site for IPSA's world congress in 1979, but also Rio de Janeiro and Paris as future sites. Finally, several questions, deleted in the short questionnaire sent to nonregistrants, were intended to find out how those who participated in the Moscow meetings evaluated the congress as a whole and their own personal experiences.

The questionnaires were mailed to respondents during the latter part of August 1980 (with follow-up questionnaires sent in mid-January 1981 to those who had not yet responded). Members of the samples in the United States received postage-free envelopes in which to return the completed questionnaires, but those outside the United States were asked themselves to cover return-postage costs. There can be little doubt about the negative impact that the latter procedure had on the rate of response (and were we to conduct another such survey we would search for better ways to encourage responsiveness from political scientists outside the United States). In fact, however, our non-U.S. colleagues were very cooperative. Their rate of return was very respectable for surveys of this kind.

General Questions for Exploration

In the following chapters we shall concentrate on the evidence provided by individual respondents, with emphasis on the following concerns.

Individual characteristics and perceptions. Individuals attending the same meeting will often go away with widely differing explanations of what happened and why. This is due in part to the particular circumstances encountered by each individual, and in part to the qualities that participants bring to the meeting in the first place. Scientists with considerable professional and international activity and status, we might anticipate, will be more likely than others to stress the scientific aspect of an international scientific congress, to be skeptical about the effects of any possible politicization, and to understand better the argument for the international institutionalization of their scientific discipline.

Functions. Of particular interest are the uses participants make of an ISC, the functions they see it serving for other actors in the scientific consociation, and the rankings they give the various functions in terms of priorities. To take but one example from the array outlined earlier, we may presume scientific communication to be functional for the individual scientist's learning. What aspects of a congress facilitate or hinder this process? One way to approach the question is to compare the participants' prior expectations about what they will find at a congress with their actual experiences. Another is to examine the extent to which the experience of attending a congress changes the participants' scientific outlook or even their views of the host country and its people. A related approach is similar to Sherlock Holmes's "curious incident of the dog in the night-time," the dog that did not bark. What functions do analysts detect but congress participants do not mention? Are the analysts off-base in their conclusions, or are these in fact latent functions necessary for the effective operation of some actor?

Subsequent behavior. Do participants actually use the opportunities they have at an international scientific congress to expand their intellectual horizons? That is, do they establish contacts with colleagues from other countries, learn something that changes the orientation or otherwise improves the quality of their research, and/or subsequently keep in touch with colleagues they first met at the congress? Here we might hypothesize that scientists who are already well known in the profession and who frequently travel overseas to conduct research and attend conferences tend to go to an international congress for different reasons and to benefit in different ways than do their colleagues with less professional status and international experience.

Perceived functionality for others. Recognizing their limitations in this respect, we might expect that those who have attended an ISC have some notion of its utility for the disciplinary association that organized it, the country that hosted it, and, perhaps, global society as a whole. Of special interest, given the location of IPSA's world congress of 1979, is the question of political functionality: Does it make a difference—to the participants, to the association, to various national governments—where international scientific congresses take place? The answer to this question also has a bearing on the value such ISCs have for global society.

Organizational principles. Answers to such questions can not only contribute to the study of international scientific associations as transnational actors but can also provide information of practical value to organizers of future international scientific congresses. For example, what are the most effective organizational structures and procedures for facilitating scientific communication and exchange? Should we wish to maximize some other value, such as further international institutionalization of a scientific discipline, how might we go about doing it? What kinds of scientific communication problems occur in such congresses, and what can be done to eliminate them? Clearly, more comparative research on ISCs is needed. This study makes a start by providing empirical evidence aimed at clarifying the many functions of ISCs, identifying their advantages and disadvantages as a means of scientific communication, and suggesting areas in which they may be improved in the future.

This study probes the functionality of international scientific congresses for the various actors identified above. First, however, we must place the study in its context. Chapter 2 accordingly looks at the International Political Science Association and its world congresses, most particularly the Moscow world congress of 1979. Succeeding chapters address the issues outlined above. Chapter 3 profiles the respondents to the survey and what they perceive to be the functions of international political science congresses for themselves and others. The Moscow congress's scientific impact is the more specific subject of Chapter 4. It examines what participants expected the meetings to be like and how they actually found them, what they learned about the Soviet Union and its people, what they gained from scientific networking, and how the meetings affected their work. It also raises the question of how IPSA and similar associations might alter their congresses to enhance this function. Chapter 5 focuses on the functionality of ISCs for national governments, most particularly the political aspects of the Moscow world congress: how respondents dealt with the call to boycott the meetings, what they feel about holding meetings in the Soviet Union, and the extent to which they saw politics intruding into the congress's sessions. The concluding Chapter 6 asks what the analysis has taught us about ISCs and explores how we might improve them in the future.

Notes

1. We are using the term "function" in the sense of "the action for which a person or thing is specially fitted or used or for which a thing exists" (*Webster's New Collegiate Dictionary*). This usage includes Merton's (1957: 51) *manifest* functions, which "are those objective consequences contributing to the adjustment or adaptation of the system which are intended and recognized by participants in the system," and *latent* functions, or "those

which are neither intended nor recognized." Implicit in this terminology is our acceptance of the idea of functional analysis, which Merton (1957: 47) has defined as the "practice of interpreting data by establishing their consequences for larger structures in which they are implicated" (see also Cancian, 1968; and Levy, 1968).

2. By the term "science" we mean to suggest both an outcome (in the sense of "systematized knowledge," as defined in *Webster's New Collegiate Dictionary*) and a process (in the sense of Kuhn's [1970: 10] "normal science," that is, "research firmly based upon one or more past scientific achievements, achievements that some particular scientific community acknowledges for a time as supplying the foundation for its further practice").

3. A society in which a particular social myth about science as a whole and individual scientific disciplines dominates may well be able to institutionalize the order that myth specifies. "Full institutionalization" of the Western scientific order was achieved, in Bernard Barber's (1968: 96) words, "when universities, various governmental organizations, and many industrial firms recognized the great need for science, and established regular and permanent roles and careers for scientists."

4. Early explorations in the sociology of science (e.g., Merton, 1942) saw the "ethos" of science in terms of interlocked cognitions defining the research framework of the discipline, norms indicating what values scientists are "supposed" to hold as scientists, and behaviors appropriate for scientists acting both as individuals and as an aggregate. The argument that the entire scientific community shared this ethos gave it legitimacy and enabled the community to exert social controls on its behalf. "Strict implementation" of "sets of formal rules," these studies assumed, "guarantees an undistorted revelation of the real physical world" (Mulkay, 1979: 95). The revisionist position on the scientific order is pluralistic. It sees not one but an array of "scientific orders," any one of which may enjoy varying support in a given society (which does not imply equal validity). It thus shifts the focus of attention from (idealized) scientists trying to unlock the unambiguous secrets of nature to the interaction between society (with its social myths) and scientists seeking to interpret their findings. Just as "objects present themselves differently to scientists in different social settings," so, too, "social resources enter into the structure of scientific assertions and conclusions" (Mulkay, 1979: 5).

5. A "consociation" is "an ecological community with a single dominant" (*Webster's New Collegiate Dictionary*). It includes, as noted below, not only a scientific community or "practitioners of a scientific specialty" (Kuhn, 1970: 177) but also individuals acting on behalf of other structures for which the particular scientific discipline is significantly relevant.

6. We are treating the scientific discipline (e.g., chemistry) as an institution in the sociological sense, and disciplinary associations as the structures (or agents) that speak or would speak for them.

7. Since Fighiera extrapolated the data on IGOs from the number of meetings held by the United Nations, they are not directly comparable to those shown in Table 1.1.

8. The United Nations Educational, Scientific and Cultural Organization conducted from 1951 to 1953 a major interdisciplinary study of the management and operation of international conferences, which sought to find out more about the factors that encourage and inhibit effective international decisionmaking through the conference process (Sharp, 1950; Soddy, 1953; UNESCO, 1953). Only one of the systematic case studies in this project analyzed a conference of a nongovernmental organization. Another surge of enthusiasm for the subject came more than two decades later in response to the series of global conferences initiated by the UN General Assembly to consider various economic and social problems. These studies were concerned with the effectiveness of such massive gatherings for making decisions on international policies and the nature of that decisionmaking process (see, for example, Weiss and Jordan, 1976).

9. We shall not discuss either subnational and subdisciplinary associations or supranational regional associations. Our assumption is that their goals and behaviors resemble those of national associations, albeit on a different scale.

10. The function this competitiveness serves for the nation-state is discussed in the next section.

11. Thus, in Bernard Barber's words: "Scientific knowledge is power, that is, power to adjust more or less satisfactorily to the nonsocial environment and to the internal and external social environment. . . . Whatever their values in regard to science, [powerful modern industrial societies] feel an urgent need to use it to strengthen their national defense, promote industrial and agricultural growth, and improve the health of their populations. . . . Finally, the nonindustrial or underdeveloped societies of the present also push the acquisition of science for urgent instrumental needs, to cope with 'the revolution of rising expectations' in their populations" (Barber, 1968: 94; see also Storer, 1970: 89).

12. IPSA's official tally reports 1,027 registrants from the nonsocialist world, of whom 856 actually attended the Moscow meetings. Using the latter figure, our 369 respondents who both registered for and said they participated in these meetings represent a response rate of 43 percent.

TWO

International Political Science: From Paris to Moscow (and Back)

Political science as a scientific discipline has been international since its beginnings scarcely a century ago. Its subject matter, the scientific study of politics and political phenomena, is inherently comparative across time and across nations. The diffusion of the discipline's concerns, approaches, and methodologies also reveals its internationality. What we now call political science spread from Germany and France throughout the Western world, including North America, and then after 1945, in revitalized form, back across the Atlantic and throughout the rest of the world. Not until the late 1940s, however, was there an institutional framework for political science that was truly international rather than the overseas extension of a particular school or subdisciplinary interest. The creation in 1949 of the International Political Science Association (IPSA) aimed at realizing the discipline's international dimensions.

A chief tool envisioned by IPSA's founders as a means to internationalize the discipline was a periodic world congress of political scientists. It was not the only such tool they and their successors devised. Others include international roundtables of IPSA research committees and study groups, various publications (the quarterly *International Political Science Review*, the bimonthly *International Political Science Abstracts*, a newsletter entitled *Participation*, as well as edited symposia contained in "Advances in political science: an international series"), and participation in the various activities and fora of the International Social Science Council. Yet the triennial world congress remains the jewel in IPSA's crown as far as establishing and enhancing international scientific communication within the discipline is concerned.

The development of IPSA and its world congresses epitomizes key aspects of the problématique of international scientific communication. In one sense its growth and the problems IPSA encounters are like those of any other scientific discipline organized internationally. Yet, in another sense, IPSA is unique. Its members, true to the central intellectual concerns of the political science discipline, tend to be more alert to the political context and ramifications of their international meetings than others might be toward their own. Moreover, like its national counterparts, IPSA's meetings seem to attract a few people more interested in making than studying politics. IPSA and its world congresses thus bring together some unusual political as well as the usual scientific and ancillary aspects of international scientific congresses.

Internationalization

The origin of the International Political Science Association lies in efforts of the United Nations Educational, Scientific and Cultural Organization (UNESCO) to further international research collaboration in the social sciences. Its Second General Conference, held in November-December 1947 in Mexico City, called on UNESCO's director general "to promote a study of the subject-matter and problems treated by political scientists of various countries in recent research materials," with particular emphasis on methodological aspects (UNESCO, 1949c: 28). The reasons given were the recent emergence of political science as a discipline and "hence the need for political science to reach, in the shortest possible time, the level of adjacent disciplines," problems caused by national diversity in terminology and approaches, and, most important, the desire to further "the maintenance of peace through intellectual co-operation":

> Among the many reasons why human beings have slaughtered one another, bringing untold sufferings (the most frightful are too recent to need description), some have been, and some are, purely political reasons. Whether these reasons are primary or secondary, the present tension between nations, and within many nations, is tied closely to phenomena that political scientists should know and understand.

Implicit in the study was the idea that enhancing "the degree of clarity and accuracy" with which "citizens of various states perceive the significance of their political conduct" could ease international tensions (UNESCO, 1949c: 28).

After some preliminary explorations, a project director appointed by UNESCO convened a meeting in September 1948 in Paris. Political scientists from several countries were asked to provide guidance for the study, including developing a questionnaire to be sent to political science institutes and associations around the world. They went further, however. Concluding that the time was ripe to institutionalize opportunities for international cooperation, they called for an international conference in 1949, "with the aim of launching an International Political Science Association" that would strengthen "cultural ties in their particular field of learning" (UNESCO, 1949b: 66). The Preparatory Committee they set up then turned, with UNESCO's assistance, to the task of organizing such a conference to be held a year later in Paris.[1]

Some 23 political scientists from 17 countries met in September 1949 to shape the International Political Science Association. Their first step was to draft a constitution, which would establish firmly that IPSA "should have purely scientific objectives, not excluding, however, the promotion of a more intelligent understanding of the principles of political science by the general public" (UNESCO, 1949a: 82). Article 5 of the constitution enumerated several appropriate activities:

> encouragement and development of national political science associations in countries where none yet exist; steps to secure a fuller recognition of political science as [a] distinct academic discipline; the facilitation of personal contacts among political scientists of various countries; the holding of international "round-table" discussions; the provision of a documentary and research service for members of the Association; and the widest possible dissemination of information concerning significant developments in political science teaching and research.

The association was to comprise collective members (national and regional associations), associate members (initially other international and national groups with objectives similar to IPSA's, but later including academic institutions), and individual members. As far as governance was concerned, the conference envisioned a tripartite structure:

1. The authoritative *council*, proportionally representative of the collective members (now with the addition of a number of co-opted "representatives" of research committees, otherwise underrepresented groups, and the like), meets only during the triennial world congresses to elect an IPSA president, select from among its own membership a new executive committee, and make formal decisions on items proposed by the outgoing executive committee or possibly arising from the council floor;

2. The eighteen-member *executive committee* (including the president and immediate past president) meets occasionally, usually at least once a year, between world congresses to oversee preparations for the ensuing congress, nominate a president-elect, select sites for future world congresses, and otherwise conduct the association's ongoing business; and

3. A permanent *secretariat* under the direction of the secretary general carries out the instructions of the council and executive committee, prepares meetings and agendas, communicates with members, and so forth.

Finally, the conference elected a provisional executive committee that would govern until the following September, when IPSA would hold its first world congress.[2] The constitution entered into force in 1949 after the accession of four members: Canada, France, India, and the United States.

The association has grown both numerically and geographically. From the 4 original collective members IPSA expanded to 8 by the time of its first world congress (1950) and to 18 by the time of the second (1952).[3] Today, some 39 member associations (including two regional associations, for Africa and Pacific Asia) come from all parts of the world. Table 2.1 traces the increase in the number of individual members from a modest 52 in 1952 to 1,510 at the outset of 1986. Equally impressive have been a broadened representativeness of the individual as well as national members and increased involvement of non-Western scholars in the activities of the organization. Although India was among the four founding countries and Poland joined in 1950, the association during its first years was very much under Western influence. Not until the 1960s did Third World countries and socialist countries other than Poland and Yugoslavia begin to play a significant role in the organization. By 1986 members came from 55 different countries. The composition of the council also changed markedly: The proportion of members from developed countries dropped from 79 percent in 1967 to half in 1976, to somewhat more (56%) in 1985; and the percentage of council members from developing and socialist countries rose from 15 to 24 percent and from 6 to 20 percent, respectively.

IPSA World Congresses

Attendance at the triennial congresses has also reflected the growth and geographical expansion of IPSA's membership. Some 80 scholars, representing 23 countries participated in the first congress, held in September 1950 in Zürich; 14 years later almost 500 political scientists from 43 countries attended the Geneva congress; and over 1,000 from 60 countries went to the Montréal congress in 1973, the first to be held outside Western Europe. The decisions to hold the 11th World Congress in Moscow in 1979 and the following one in Rio de Janeiro in 1982 increased the number of participants from Eastern Europe and Latin America and symbolized the enlarged geographical scope of the association. The total number of registrants at both these meetings neared 1,500. The world congress in Paris in 1985 attracted 1,763 participants.

As important as the quantitative expansion of IPSA world congresses was their substantive growth. The Zürich congress of 1950 began with Quincy Wright's presidential address, in which he said (1951: 275):

> The conditions which have brought our Association into existence are the corruption of politics by inhuman tyranny and total war which

Table 2.1 International Political Science Association, 1950-1985
Membership, Attendance at World Congresses, and Countries Represented

Date	Number of Members	Congress Location	Number of Participants	Number of Countries Represented
1950		Zürich	80	23
1952	52	Hague	220	31
1955	232	Stockholm	275	36
1958	425	Rome	320	31
1961	442	Paris	425	46
1964	420	Geneva	494	43
1967	520	Brussels	745	56
1970	510	Munich	894	46
1973	450	Montréal	1044	56
1976	532	Edinburgh	1081	56
1979	687	Moscow	1466	53
1982	1211	Rio de Janeiro	1477	49
1985	1510	Paris	1763	66
1988		Washington		

Sources: Philippart, 1970: 17, 42-57; Scohy, 1977: 21, 41-58; IPSA, *Participation*, 1,1 (January 1977): 25, 4,1 (January 1980): 13, and 7,1 (Spring 1983): 21; and the secretary general's "Three year report, 1982-1985" (August 1985) as well as "Secretary-general's report, July-December 1985" (February 1986).

have brought and may again bring disastrous consequences to all sections of the world. The purpose which inspires our Association is to eliminate these corruptions by the universal application of scientific method in dealing with political problems.

The congress, convened jointly with the International Sociological Association's first world congress, then turned to three main themes:[4] minimum conditions for an effective and permanent union of nation-states; influence of electoral systems on political life; and the citizen's part in a planned society (UNESCO, 1950a). Each theme focused on three written papers, followed by general discussion.[5] Finally, a joint roundtable with sociologists dealt with the influence of a country's ethical structure on its foreign policy, conceived in the framework of UNESCO's project on tensions that affect international understanding.

Ensuing IPSA world congresses saw the association moving slowly toward a format that would be at once flexible and stabilizing. The Hague congress of 1952 offered 57 papers in 11 roundtables organized around 3 themes—local government as a basis of and training in democracy, the role of ideologies in political change, and the political role of women—and 2 roundtables on a fourth, the UNESCO survey of teaching in political science in 12 countries (for extensive rapporteurs' reports, see UNESCO, 1953). The Stockholm congress of 1955 developed a new pattern of plenary sessions on 5 main themes followed by related sessions for specialists (with 25 papers) and, at the end of the congress, a plenary session at which rapporteurs for each theme presented their summaries (Meynaud and Reynolds, 1956). The themes were metropolitan governance, political parties, political implications of economic development programs, large and small states in international organization, and political conditions of democracy. Subsequent congresses in Rome (1958) had 6 themes and 77 papers, in Paris (1961) 5 themes and 59 papers, in Geneva (1964) 6 themes and 94 papers, and in Brussels (1967) 9 themes and 96 papers (UNESCO, 1959; Philippart, 1970: 42-62).

By this time two trends were identifiable. One was a proliferation of topics. It suggested, at least symbolically, a fragmentation of the discipline into its diverse subspecialties. To counteract such an impression, future congresses sought to emphasize a very small number of overarching themes (two in Montréal, 1973; one in Edinburgh, 1976; three in Moscow, 1979; three in Rio de Janeiro, 1982; and four in Paris, 1985) while, through the allocation of sessions, recognizing differences in specific subject matters and approaches. The Edinburgh meeting was especially interesting in this respect. The central theme, "Time, space, and politics," provided a framework within which the executive committee organized 22 sections (two-thirds of them comprising two distinct sessions each). Later program organizers identified a number of section topics appropriate to each theme and published in *Participation* brief rationales for the selection of their themes and organization of section topics.[6]

A second trend saw the emergence of subsidiary groups within IPSA that sought time outside the regular program to conduct their own sessions. Specialists' meetings appeared for the first time at the Geneva congress (1964). Some of these turned into organizational meetings for more enduring networks that would subsequently distribute newsletters, develop periodic roundtables, and ask for reserved slots on congress programs. At the Munich congress in 1970 the executive committee officially recognized two such groups: the Research Committee on Conceptual and Terminological Analysis (COCTA) and the Research Committee on Political Sociology (a joint committee with the International Sociological Association). By 1976, when their number had grown to 14, the executive committee began the process of institutionalizing the research committees (Trent, 1978). Four years later it adopted guidelines for recognizing new research committees, ensuring that they were active on a continuing basis (that is, not appearing solely every three years to claim space on the program), terminating those that were inactive, and establishing the category of "study groups" as incipient research committees. The path of growth nevertheless continues. In 1986 IPSA had 24 research committees and an equal number of study groups.

In part to control this tendency toward diffused foci at its world congresses, IPSA established a program committee in 1976. Previous practice had the executive committee, under the direction of the IPSA president, organizing the congress program and supervising its realization. Effectively, however, the main organizational burden rested on the shoulders of the president, who also had a wide variety of other administrative and representational tasks to perform. The new president elected in 1976 at the Edinburgh congress, Karl W. Deutsch (United States), agreed to serve on the condition that he could share with an independent program committee the burden of the Moscow congress. Accordingly, and with the executive committee's approval, he appointed the first such committee and a program chair. Six years later the executive committee changed IPSA's constitution to incorporate this innovation, making the program chair an appointive officer of the association and ex officio member of the executive committee.

Moscow World Congress, 1979

It was in this fluid associational setting that the IPSA program committee undertook to organize the 11th World Congress, to be held in August 1979 in Moscow. On the one hand, the task was well defined. The committee had for its guidance the precedents of 10 previous congresses. Moreover, the association's president, preceding president, secretary general (all members of the program committee), and program chair had each been directly responsible for organizing either an IPSA world congress or an annual meeting of the American or Canadian political science association. This experience made it relatively simple to proceed in a straightforward fashion.

On the other hand, the Moscow congress posed some new challenges. Establishing the freedom of action of the newly created program committee was one of them. Not all members of the current or previous executive committees saw the need for such a committee; and a few even felt that its creation had taken organizational privileges out of their own hands. This matter was resolved by creating overlapping membership (with 8 members of the executive committee plus the IPSA secretary general on the 20-person program committee), bringing the executive committee as much as possible into the program committee's communications network, and ensuring that the executive committee had opportunities to review the program committee's decisions on important questions. The procedures developed in 1976–1979 worked sufficiently well that the executive committee institutionalized them for succeeding world congresses.

A second challenge was to set up a program that was intellectually first-rate, one that would attract the world's leading political scientists to Moscow in 1979. The program committee developed the congress around three main themes. One was the *politics of peace* (Alker, 1978; Shakhnazarov, 1978; Merle, 1978). Its nine sections (each comprising two sessions) dealt with such topics as conceptions of peace, relaxation of international tensions, arms races and arms control, and the domestic politics of peace and war. A second theme, on the *politics of development and system change* (Bose, 1978), included sections on socioeconomic structures and political systems in comparative perspective, planning and its implementation, the politics of unbalanced growth, and the politics of nonalignment as a factor of development. The third theme, *cumulative growth in political knowledge since 1949* (Semenov, 1978; Ludz, 1979), looked at what political scientists had learned since the year of IPSA's founding. Individual sections explored comparative macro- and micro-analysis, systems theory, normative political theory, information systems, and related topics.

The Moscow meetings attracted more registrants and active participants than any previous IPSA world congress. As many as 1,466 political scientists attended (Table 2.2). Under the 3 main themes, section convenors organized 56 sessions. The final program scheduled for these sessions 56 chairpersons, 212 papergivers presenting a total of 177 papers (abstracted in Merritt and Smirnov, 1979-1981), and 58 discussants.[7] The congress program also included 45 sessions organized by 17 research committees and 7 study groups, and 39 special meetings, which, together, accounted for 269 scheduled papers written by 326 scholars. In all, the program listed 846 active participants (some of them, of course, acting in a double capacity as papergiver in one session and discussant in another).

A third challenge was organizing the first IPSA congress to take place in a non-Western country: the Soviet Union. With the program chair residing in the United States and the IPSA secretariat in Canada, this meant at best attenuated lines of communication between them and the Soviet organizing committee. As it turned out, however, it was not communication but international politics that intervened to make this task especially challenging.

Politics of Site Selection

Selecting the site for an international scientific congress is not a trivial matter. A selection committee must first raise a host of questions about a potential site's facilities, accessibility, and demonstrated skill in organizing congresses. It might inquire about the host country's willingness to cover some proportion of the costs for administration, travel, and the like. Increasingly, it seems, the committee must also ask essentially political questions. It must take account of the host country's policy on admitting

INTERNATIONAL POLITICAL SCIENCE 37

Table 2.2 Participation at IPSA World Congress, 1979

Country	Partici-pants No.	%	Program Comm. Sessions Con	Pap	Dis	Res/St Groups Sessions Con	Pap	Dis	Special Meetings Con	Pap	Dis	All Sessions Convener No.	%	All Sessions Papergiver No.	%	All Sessions Discuss. No.	%
Eastern Europe																	
Soviet Union	260	18	4	16	2	2	7	1	6	11	6	12	8	34	6	9	5
Bulgaria	50	3	-	-	1	-	-	-	-	-	-	-	-	-	-	1	1
Czechoslovakia	50	3	1	4	1	-	-	-	-	-	1	1	1	4	1	2	1
Germany (GDR)	50	3	1	5	3	-	-	1	-	2	-	1	1	7	1	4	2
Hungary	50	3	1	2	2	-	-	-	-	2	1	1	1	4	1	3	2
Poland	50	3	2	2	1	5	5	2	-	3	2	7	5	10	2	5	3
Romania	50	3	2	7	1	-	3	2	1	1	1	3	2	11	2	4	2
Yugoslavia	50	3	3	4	1	2	4	1	2	3	2	5	4	11	2	2	1
	610	42	14	40	11	7	19	6	9	22	13	30	21	81	15	30	18
North America																	
United States	229	16	10	59	15	15	64	15	13	48	11	38	27	171	32	41	25
Canada	51	3	3	19	3	4	8	3	4	10	1	11	8	37	7	7	4
	280	19	13	78	18	19	72	18	17	58	12	49	35	208	39	48	29
Western Europe																	
Germany (FRG)	64	4	3	12	2	2	7	5	3	11	1	8	6	30	6	8	5
France	42	3	3	2	2	-	5	1	2	5	4	5	4	12	2	7	4
Sweden	37	3	1	1	4	-	7	3	-	5	1	1	1	13	2	8	5
Spain	34	2	-	4	-	-	-	1	-	3	1	3	2	7	1	2	1
United Kingdom	34	2	3	4	-	4	7	5	3	3	5	10	7	14	3	10	6
Netherlands	32	2	-	4	-	-	3	2	-	2	-	-	-	9	2	2	1
Israel	29	2	1	4	-	1	3	1	2	2	1	4	3	9	2	2	1
Turkey	22	2	1	5	1	1	2	-	-	1	1	2	1	8	1	1	1
Norway	21	1	-	3	-	1	3	1	-	-	-	1	1	6	1	2	1
Finland	20	1	2	7	2	1	2	1	-	6	3	2	1	15	3	6	4
Belgium	15	1	-	-	-	1	3	-	-	-	1	1	1	3	1	1	1

Table 2.2—continued

Country	Partici- pants No.	%	Program Comm. Sessions Con	Pap	Dis	Res/St Groups Sessions Con	Pap	Dis	Special Meetings Con	Pap	Dis	All Sessions Convener No.	%	Papergiver No.	%	Discuss. No.	%
Western Europe—continued																	
Denmark	12	1	1	4	-	-	4	-	-	-	1	1	1	8	1	1	1
Italy	12	1	1	1	-	-	7	-	-	1	1	1	1	9	2	1	1
Switzerland	11	1	2	2	-	1	1	1	-	2	1	3	2	5	1	1	1
Greece	4	*	-	-	-	-	1	-	-	-	-	-	-	2	*	-	-
Ireland	3	*	-	-	-	-	1	-	-	-	-	-	-	-	-	-	-
Luxembourg	2	*	-	-	-	1	2	1	-	-	1	1	1	2	*	2	1
Austria	2	*	-	-	-	-	-	-	-	-	-	2	1	1	*	-	-
	395	27	19	53	11	13	58	22	13	42	20	45	33	153	28	53	32
Asia and Pacific																	
India	32	2	4	10	3	3	4	4	-	9	4	7	5	23	4	11	7
Japan	30	2	-	6	2	-	5	1	1	2	-	1	1	13	2	3	2
Korea (South)	21	1	-	9	5	-	4	-	-	-	-	-	-	13	2	5	3
Australia	6	*	-	-	-	-	2	-	-	3	1	-	-	5	1	1	1
New Zealand	3	*	-	-	-	-	1	-	-	1	-	-	-	2	*	-	-
Thailand	2	*	-	-	-	-	-	-	-	-	-	-	-	-	-	1	1
Vietnam	2	*	-	-	-	-	-	-	-	-	-	-	-	1	*	-	-
Hong Kong	1	*	-	-	-	-	1	-	-	-	-	-	-	-	-	-	-
Indonesia	1	*	-	1	1	-	-	-	-	-	-	-	-	2	*	1	1
Malaysia	1	*	-	-	-	-	1	-	-	-	-	-	-	-	-	-	-
Pakistan	1	*	-	-	-	-	-	2	-	-	-	-	-	2	*	1	1
Philippines	1	*	-	-	-	-	-	-	-	-	-	-	-	-	-	-	-
Singapore	1	*	-	-	-	-	-	-	-	-	-	-	-	-	-	-	-
	102	7	4	26	11	3	20	7	1	15	6	8	6	61	11	24	14

INTERNATIONAL POLITICAL SCIENCE   39

Africa and Middle East																	
Nigeria	4	*	-	2	1	2	-	3	-	1	-	3	2	6	1	1	1
Algeria	2	*	-	-	-	-	3	-	-	1	-	1	1	-	-	-	-
Cameroun	1	*	1	-	-	-	1	-	-	-	-	1	-	1	*	-	-
Ivory Coast	1	*	-	-	-	-	-	-	-	-	-	-	-	-	-	-	-
Jordan	1	*	-	-	-	-	-	-	-	-	-	-	-	-	-	-	-
Sierra Leone	1	*	-	-	-	-	-	-	-	-	-	-	-	-	-	-	-
	10	1	1	2	1	2	4	-	1	1	-	4	3	7	1	1	1
Latin America																	
Mexico	47	3	-	3	2	-	-	-	-	-	-	-	-	3	1	2	1
Brazil	11	1	3	3	-	-	4	1	-	1	2	3	2	8	1	3	2
Venezuela	5	*	-	-	-	-	-	-	-	1	-	-	-	1	*	-	-
Argentina	3	*	-	1	1	1	-	-	-	1	-	1	-	1	*	1	1
Cuba	2	*	-	-	-	-	-	-	-	-	-	-	-	-	-	-	-
Chile	1	*	-	-	-	-	2	-	-	-	-	-	-	2	*	1	1
	69	5	3	7	4	1	6	1	-	2	2	4	3	15	3	7	4
Other	-	-	2	6	2	-	5	1	-	2	-	2	1	13	2	3	2
	1466	100	56	212	58	45	184	55	41	142	53	142	100	538	100	166	100
Summary																	
Eastern Europe	610	42	14	40	11	7	19	6	9	22	13	30	21	81	15	30	18
North America	280	19	13	78	18	19	72	18	17	58	12	49	35	208	39	48	29
Other Western	382	26	18	48	10	12	59	22	13	45	20	43	30	152	28	52	31
Third World	194	13	11	46	19	7	34	9	2	17	8	20	14	97	18	36	22
	1466	100	56	212	58	45	184	55	41	142	53	142	100	538	100	166	100

Source: *Participation*, 4, 1 (January 1980): 13; and *IPSA World Congress Program*, 1979.

*Less than 0.5 percent; columns may not add to 100 because of rounding error.

nationals of certain countries and the possible political uses to which it may put a congress. Like the sports world, the scientific world has seen countries shamelessly use such events to tout the virtues of their own political systems or national character. IPSA officers are keenly aware that this kind of behavior can adversely affect the success of an international scientific congress.

Such political considerations play a role not only for members of selection committees but also for individual scientists who must decide whether or not to attend a particular congress. At one pole are those who are prepared to go any place where they can freely discuss their research and exchange information. They represent the traditional view that science is (or ought to be) above politics and that the value of scientific communication transcends ideological differences no less than national boundaries. The discipline of political science will also advance, according to this line of thinking, as perspectives broaden. It thus makes sense to hold meetings precisely in those places where scholars pursue lines of inquiry and use methodologies different from our own. Should they choose not to learn from us, we can at least learn from them and hence improve the breadth and quality of our own scientific work.

At the other extreme are scientists for whom political conditions are very important when choosing a site for a congress or deciding about their own attendance. One such point of view insists that scientific communication and exchange, which to flourish require an open setting, are ipso facto inhibited in a repressive political system. Accordingly, a decision to hold a scientific meeting in such a system does not serve the interests of science—but may legitimize and/or reward the repressive régime by providing tourist revenues and conferring status, as well as providing propaganda opportunities for a government that violates basic human rights. It may also put a stamp of international acceptance on a régime that pursues an aggressive foreign policy. It follows, in this view, that individual scientists should refuse to attend congresses held in these countries.

An alternative, and equally political, point of view argues that holding scientific meetings in such a country may contribute to its liberalization, to opening it up for free discourse. This stance rejects boycotts, which only increase the country's isolation in the international arena and encourage its repressive behavior. Enhancing communication through scientific meetings in such a country may, by contrast, help to reduce tensions and thereby contribute to a more stable international environment.

Not surprisingly, given its essential intellectual concerns, the International Political Science Association has seen international politics crop up in decisions about sites for its triennial world congresses. This was not a serious problem before the late 1970s. Some members questioned the appropriateness of particular sites—Munich in 1970 because of its historical associations, Montréal in 1973 because of a potential danger to Israeli scholars, and Edinburgh in 1976 because of the possibility that Scottish nationalists might disrupt the planned sessions on devolution—but their voices were few in number, the problems they foresaw manageable, and the tone of argumentation not very convincing. Decisions reached in 1976 to hold IPSA's next world congresses in Moscow and Rio de Janeiro raised a few more eyebrows.

What is political about selecting a site for an ISC? The answer to this query can shed light on the much broader question of the political ramifications of international scientific cooperation. As Francis Bacon and many after him have observed, knowledge is power. This truism has become more accurate as societies move toward ever more complex industrial bases that demand effective scientific research and development. Governments have had to decide for themselves when freedom of information endangers their competitive position vis-à-vis other states in the global arena or even their national security. A logical extension of government secrecy acts is the effort to prevent scientific interchanges that can unduly advantage one's competitors. Thus, during the hottest days of the cold war, governments did not grant entry to scholars from the "other side" and sharply limited the free flow of scientific publications. Nor were they prepared to grant passports to those among their own citizens who wished to study or attend conferences in hostile countries.

Steps toward international relaxation in the 1970s opened up new possibilities for international scientific cooperation, including joint U.S.-Soviet ventures in outer space. But the hostility of an earlier decade was not forgotten, and few were willing to interpret the new setting of peaceful coexistence and competition as one in which the superpowers had ceased jockeying for a position of scientific supremacy. The relaxation also turned what had been a practical constraint into opportunities laden with moral overtones. In the 1950s, as some scientists—not all of them in the West—pointed out, it had not been possible to attend a truly scientific international congress in the Soviet Union. Now that it was possible, was it right to go to a country which, in their opinion, controlled information, persecuted dissidents, and maintained its imperium over Eastern Europe? Other scientists raised similar questions about visiting the United States, with its legacy of McCarthyism, Vietnam, and the CIA, or countries in the Third World with records of military dictatorship and popular oppression.

Decisions by IPSA to hold its world congresses of 1979 in Moscow and 1982 in Rio de Janeiro forced political scientists to come to terms with such questions. They faced a condition, not a theory. Whether intended or not, the decisions certified that, as far as IPSA was concerned, Soviet and Brazilian political science had come of age. The decisions made clear the fact that IPSA would not impose political conditions on any one country, such as the

Soviet Union or Brazil, that it was unwilling to impose on others. What was less clear was the extent to which national associations and individual political scientists—especially those outside the socialist world—would accept the implications of these decisions. Did they, do they, view political principles as ascendant over the ideal of unbounded scientific cooperation?

In short, although the potential for conflict has always existed in IPSA decisions about where its world congresses should be held, and although rumblings of dissatisfaction had been heard before, it was not really until IPSA decided to go to Moscow for its world congress of 1979 that the political implications of such decisions became manifest. Virtually no dispute at all attended the initial decision. Subsequently, however, it erupted in a way that challenged some basic principles underlying the association's viability as a truly international scientific body.

Choosing Moscow

The International Political Science Association does not have a highly elaborated procedure for selecting sites for its triennial world congresses. National associations interested in hosting a congress submit invitations to IPSA's executive committee, which in turn decides which invitation to accept.

Before accepting an invitation, however, the IPSA executive committee ascertains that the host country can meet certain "normal" conditions. These include free access to the congress for all bona fide political scientists (at least those from countries that are collective members of the association), free discussion at the congress, agreement to the principle that the association and its committees make all programmatic decisions, and some minimal financial guarantees (such as providing travel funds for participants from the Third World and simultaneous translation for at least the plenary sessions). As noted earlier, the executive committee must also satisfy itself that the host country has appropriate facilities for the congress: an ample number of meeting rooms, available hotels at various price ranges (including, if possible, inexpensive dormitory space for graduate students and others), technical capabilities such as a staff that will be made available for organizing the congress, and, if necessary, formal support from the host country's government and/or national academy of science.

In practice, the process of selecting a site can entail complex negotiations. First of all, only rarely are national associations competing to host an IPSA world congress. The problem is more one of persuading national associations to submit invitations. The IPSA world congress in 1970 almost collapsed when the British association withdrew its invitation at virtually the last minute; only a hastily arranged agreement by the West

German association to host the meeting at Munich saved it. Typically, the IPSA executive committee must lobby its associational members to persuade them that the advantages of hosting a world congress—advantages such as the common weal of international political science, an opportunity for the host country's young scholars to interact with a vast array of experts, and prestige for the host association—are worth its costs.

Second, working out acceptable conditions can raise a number of delicate problems. Every national association must function within constraints set by its government; and, while the association may try to make necessary arrangements with its government, in the last analysis it does not control either what the government sets as policy or how petty officials such as customs agents interpret this policy. To take actual examples, neither the American Political Science Association nor the Canadian Political Science Association can absolutely *guarantee* that officials of its government will not bar entry to a communist or homosexual wishing to attend an international scientific meeting.[8] Were the IPSA executive committee to demand an ironclad guarantee of this sort, it would be demanding something it cannot obtain. What the executive committee can demand is an assurance on the part of the host association that it will do everything possible to secure the admission of bona fide political scientists—again, at least those from IPSA's collective members—and a recognition by both parties that, should the host association's government violate this principle, IPSA will cancel the meeting, even on short notice.

The complications entailed in locating an appropriate site have meant in practice that the task devolves upon the IPSA president and secretary general. Initiatives are discussed with the executive committee; and ultimately it is the latter body that makes the final decision to hold a world congress in a particular city. The mode of decisionmaking on the question has in the past been collegial—especially since the task has been more frequently to find a national association willing to host a world congress than to select one from among many proffered sites.

The Decision

At its meeting in summer 1974 the IPSA executive committee considered the question of where to hold its world congress of 1979. Only the representative of the Rumanian Political Science Association had submitted a tentative offer. The executive committee encouraged the Rumanian representative to pursue the question with his national association and government, and return to the executive committee meeting in summer 1975 with a formal invitation. The amount of time available proved to be too short for this to be done. (A Rumanian invitation eventually arrived, but only after the IPSA president had sent to executive committee members a request for advice on a Soviet invitation which had been submitted in the meantime.)

Without the Rumanian invitation in hand, the executive committee was seriously concerned when it met in summer 1975 about the site for its world congress a mere 4 years hence. A Brazilian member of the executive committee, Candido Mendes, indicated that he could secure an invitation from his national association to hold the world congress in Rio de Janeiro. When, however, Vladimir Toumanov proposed Moscow as a site, Mendes deferred with the observation that, if it proved to be impossible to hold the meeting in Moscow, he would again offer Rio as the site for 1979. Since previous informal offers from Soviet representatives had not turned into formal invitations, evidently few members of the executive committee expected that one would be forthcoming for 1979.

As it turned out, in December 1975 the IPSA president, Jean A. Laponce of Canada, received a formal Soviet invitation. With no others in sight, and with the Brazilian offer deferred, he circulated the invitation to executive committee members with the request that they consider it, discuss it with their national associations, and be prepared to vote on it at their next meeting in August 1976, on the day before the opening of the Edinburgh world congress. The executive committee voted unanimously at that meeting to accept both the Soviet invitation to hold a world congress in Moscow in August 1979 and the Brazilian invitation for 1982.

Questions were raised retrospectively about the way in which that decision was made. The answers are several. On the one hand, in summer 1975 the IPSA executive committee did not have a serious candidate to host the meeting in 1979. The Rumanian invitation had not yet materialized, and the suggestions of Rio de Janeiro and Moscow were really straws in the wind. Members of the executive committee were very conscious of the near collapse of their world congress in 1970; and the association's president and past presidents—Laponce, Carl J. Friedrich of the United States, and Stein Rokkan of Norway—had not met with success in their efforts to drum up a site. The receipt of the Soviet invitation was viewed with relief rather than apprehension. This was especially so since Soviet representatives agreed orally to provide travel grants for Third World participants equivalent to the amount given by the Canadian government for the Montréal world congress in 1973, and agreed in writing both to guarantee free access to the Moscow meetings for all members of national associations then affiliated with IPSA and to ensure that the meetings themselves would, as in the past, enjoy complete freedom of discussion.

On the other hand, IPSA executive committee members could not see any particular reason why the world congress should *not* be held in Moscow. If there were moral or other objections to the status of full equality enjoyed by the Soviet Political Science Association as a member association of

IPSA, these objections should have been expressed in 1955 when membership was granted and not two decades afterwards, when the Soviet association sought to exercise one of the rights of membership. Moreover, although executive committee members had long sought to hold a world congress in Eastern Europe, all previous efforts to do so had come to naught. The notion of geographic equity in site selection suggested that Moscow might well be an appropriate site. Besides, as some European members of the executive committee pointed out, postponing the meeting in Rio de Janeiro was a good idea on the grounds of cost alone, since the city is far distant from the universities and research organizations housing most of the association's members. Still others viewed an IPSA world congress in Moscow as a logical step in the light of the Helsinki accords and even as one that might further the process of global détente.

Negotiations and Confrontations

After the IPSA council, representing the member associations, had met and raised no objection to the executive committee's decision to hold the world congress in Moscow in 1979, the newly elected IPSA president, Karl W. Deutsch of the United States, set in motion the organizational work discussed earlier. The ensuing months also saw a number of practical issues arise as the principles agreed to in 1976 were made operational. Perhaps the most important of these was ensuring that all bona fide political scientists would secure visas from Soviet authorities early enough to make travel plans in a timely fashion. Recent difficulties, especially on the part of Israeli delegations seeking to attend scientific congresses in the Soviet Union, led to lengthy talks and a series of mutual assurances on the part of the IPSA executive committee and the Soviet organizing committee. Deutsch, speaking also on behalf of the executive committee, made it clear that denial of visas in violation of these mutual understandings would lead him to cancel the world congress scheduled for 1979 or else transfer it to another site. This turned out not to be necessary—despite a near breakdown in communications that delayed the Israeli visas until virtually the last minute.[9]

Far more serious was the dispute that erupted because of the Soviet treatment of dissident scholars. Soviet authorities arrested Yuri Fyodorovich Orlov and Alexander Ginsburg in February 1977 and Anatoly Sharansky a month later. Orlov was sentenced to a prison term in May 1978, Ginsburg and Sharansky in July 1978. The view that these arrests and trials were clear-cut violations of the Helsinki accords and basic principles of human rights led a number of political scientists in the West to question seriously the appropriateness of holding an international scientific congress in Moscow, and to ask other political scientists to search their consciences before deciding if they would attend such a meeting.[10] (It is quite likely, we might note in passing, that the substantive questions implicit in this line of argument would have arisen even in the absence of any such Soviet actions. What many saw as outright political persecution of scientists nonetheless lent virulence to the issue.)

The issue, plain and simple, focused on the political preconditions IPSA should impose on potential hosts of world congresses. Doubts were expressed about the sincerity of Soviet guarantees of free access and free discussion (and, indeed, even about whether there was a credible political science in the Soviet Union!). Some political scientists in the United States and elsewhere argued that the demands of solidarity with persecuted scientists, which would have IPSA cancel or at least have the national associations boycott the Moscow world congress, outweighed any potential benefits that could be derived from participation. Calling off or boycotting the meetings, in this view, would symbolically demonstrate to the Soviet Union that scientists in the rest of the world would neither tolerate Soviet persecution nor cooperate with the Soviet government when it engaged in such behavior, withhold from the Soviet Union the rewards attendant upon hosting an IPSA world congress, and possibly even force Soviet authorities to end their pressure on dissidents.

Others argued that withdrawing the world congress from Moscow was neither a desirable move nor an effective sanction on Soviet behavior. Indeed, they said, such a step could easily destroy the gains IPSA had made in its three decades of existence and perhaps even the association itself. At a minimum, a boycott would split IPSA along East-West lines—and it was by no means certain that the Third World would follow the West in recreating an *international* political science association. Would punishing or at least withholding rewards from the Soviet Union in fact affect Soviet behavior? Probably not, this line of argument responded, given past evidence about what losses in terms of world public opinion the Soviet government was prepared to accept if it saw basic political values at stake. The imposition of political preconditions would more generally set a precedent that might make it difficult in the future to find any acceptable site for an IPSA world congress. If the principle were accepted with respect to the Soviet Union, for instance, would not charges of "institutionalized racism" in the United States or suppression by the United Kingdom of "legitimate" Irish interests in Ulster rule out those countries as potential sites for future IPSA world congresses?

The issue reached a head in summer 1978, after the sentencing of Ginsburg and Sharansky. At its meeting in the last week of August in Rio de Janeiro, the IPSA executive committee drafted a lengthy resolution which, after taking note of "the trials and incarceration of political dissenters in the Soviet Union on issues which many consider to be tied to basic questions of human rights," went on to explain why it was nevertheless important to continue planning for the meeting in Moscow, and to cite the continued importance of "freedom of access, communication, speech, and debate" as conditions for actually holding the Moscow world congress.[11] During the following week the council of the American Political Science Association and its general membership meeting rejected resolutions calling for a boycott and accepted in their place one creating a special APSA advisory committee. Its tasks were to ensure that the conditions set by IPSA were being met in Moscow and to advise the APSA membership should the Soviet Union violate those principles.[12] (Other national associations did not discuss seriously the possibility of boycotting the Moscow world congress.)

The IPSA and APSA resolutions cleared the air in one sense: They established firmly that, barring some major and unforeseen event, the world congress of 1979 would take place as scheduled in Moscow. They did not, however, resolve the central issue at dispute. The sentiment persisted in some quarters that it was morally wrong to attend the congress. Doubtless some political scientists decided on this account not to apply for a place on the program; and a trio of leading political scientists in the United States even circulated a letter asking their colleagues to boycott the meetings. (As far as the IPSA program chair could discern, however, only one person who was listed in the preliminary program actually asked that, pursuant to the call for a boycott, his name be withdrawn.) Nor did the resolutions satisfactorily answer the question of whether or not decisions on sites for IPSA world congresses should or even could be used as sanctions. Least of all did the modus vivendi achieved in summer 1978 mean that participants in the Moscow world congress would later be of one mind about its conduct and consequences (see Chapter 5).

Some Questions for Research

Chapter 1 listed several questions of interest to theory and practice regarding international scientific congresses in general. The fact that the ISC studied here dealt with political scientists enables us to pose some of these questions a bit more precisely in their context. On the one hand, since in most respects IPSA world congresses conform to the basic format of other ISCs and perform the same tasks more or less imperfectly, the Moscow meetings can be seen as a case study of the more general phenomenon of international scientific congresses. On the other hand, however, IPSA's world congress in Moscow was sufficiently different that it invites special attention. Its underlying political tensions serve to highlight that particular aspect of other congresses as well.

Individual Scientists

Characteristics. The findings of Ladd and Lipset (1978) cited earlier regarding the American professoriat led us to expect that the participants at the IPSA congress in Moscow would be highly unrepresentative of the profession as a whole—to have traveled more, published more, and attended more international meetings than the average political scientist. To test this hypothesis we compared the biographical characteristics and attitudes of participants in the Moscow congress with those of a comparable sample chosen at random among North American political scientists who did not go to Moscow in 1979. We were particularly interested in the relationship between the participants' level of professional activity and international experience and their views on the purposes of ISCs and the impact of the IPSA congress in 1979.

An hypothesis our data did not allow us to test, but for which we shall assume prima facie validity, is that the participants, being political scientists, were more alert than others might be to political ramifications of the congress. Since we did not send questionnaires to scholars from other disciplines, and no directly comparable study exists, we cannot be completely sure that the assumption is accurate. It nonetheless stands to reason. Political scientists may be no more attuned than others to the overt politics of an international congress—whether or not, for example, the host country discriminates against scholars from some other country, and what practical consequences participants should draw from a finding that discrimination does exist. Yet the more subtle political behavior of a host country may be more apparent to trained political scientists than to others.

Perceived functions. We addressed this question by asking our respondents both why they did or did not participate in national and international congresses, especially the IPSA meetings in Moscow, and what value such congresses have for individual participants. "At first sight," a respected Dutch political scientist (Barents, 1959: 1092) noted of the Rome world congress,

> it seems paradoxical that hundreds of political scientists should have travelled to Rome to hear about pressure groups in Kamchatka or about the strange ways of public administration in Ruritania; yet I was time and again struck by the sudden flashes of insight and the unexpected doses of human interest that some of these interventions provided.

Such arguments and partial data led us to expect that a preponderance of respondents would both cite as the major function of ISCs some aspect of the process of scientific communication and indicate a scientific reason for attending the Moscow congress. We also expected that those who went to

Moscow would express a more scientific orientation than those who did not. We did not expect respondents to place great weight on the personal, nonscientific, or careerist advantages of attending the IPSA meetings in Moscow. Recognizing that questionnaires distributed by mail were not an appropriate instrument for ascertaining the participants' "true" motives, we did not press them too hard on this question. We simply asked them about the value of national and international congresses for the individual participant.[13]

Behavioral change. If it is true, as many people say, that the key function of an international scientific congress is scientific communication, then the experience of attending the congress should change in some way the participants' scientific outlook or modus operandi. Did participants actually use the opportunities they had in Moscow to expand their intellectual horizons? That is, did they establish contacts with colleagues from other countries, learn something that changed the orientation or otherwise contributed to the quality of their research, and/or subsequently keep in touch with colleagues first met at the congress? We hypothesized that those who were already well known in the profession and who frequently traveled to conduct research and attend conferences tend to go to an international congress for different reasons and to benefit in different ways than do their colleagues with less professional status and international experience.

Research Organizations

We did not expect our respondents to pay much attention to the value of the IPSA world congress for the universities and other organizations that employ them. The Western tradition of scholarship stresses the accomplishments of the scholar as an individual rather than as a representative of some organization.[14] Individual participants might note institutional affiliations but will not dwell on them to any great extent. (Had we circulated questionnaires among political scientists from socialist countries that stress a more collectivist orientation, we might have discovered significant differences on this score.)

Disciplinary Associations

Among the several scientific associations that stand to gain or lose from various aspects of an international scientific congress, the most prominent are the national association hosting the congress and the international association that organized it. The former may profit in terms of greater visibility or prestige. Archie Brown (1984: 322-323), outlining the struggles of Soviet political scientists to gain a measure of permanent status for their fledgling Soviet Political Science Association, wrote:

> A considerable stimulus to the development of political science in the USSR was the holding of the eleventh world congress of the International Political Science Association in Moscow in 1979. The fact that this was widely reported in the Soviet press (including a message of welcome to the participants from Leonid Brezhnev on the front page of *Pravda*), radio and television helped further to legitimise both the academic study of politics and the idea that there could be constructive and good-tempered discussion with Western scholars (who tended to be described, at least for the duration of the congress, as "non-Marxist" rather than "bourgeois" political scientists) even on such a sensitive subject.

(Leading political scientists in Brazil and, more generally, Latin America hoped that the IPSA world congress held in 1982 in Rio de Janeiro would have a similar effect.) An interesting question is whether or not the respondents from nonsocialist countries sensed the concerns and needs of the Soviet association. We expected that they would not. Without the concrete knowledge that comes from study of or direct contact with the Soviet association, most commenting on this point might simply be transferring their understanding of what their own national associations might gain or lose.

Moreover, since relatively few respondents were part of IPSA's decisionmaking structure, it seemed unlikely that many would probe deeply into the functionality for the association of its world congress. We nevertheless anticipated that respondents with substantial experience at IPSA world congresses would be more likely than others to recognize the value of the Moscow meetings for that body.

National Governments

Earlier we noted that the country hosting an ISC normally obtains certain advantages and incurs certain costs. The IPSA world congress in Moscow, of course, was not a "normal" international scientific congress in at least its political dimension. What distinguishes it was the opening it provided for national and international politics to intrude overtly into international political science. The possibility of a boycott, denial of visas to the political scientists of one or another country, or even some disruption at the meetings themselves lent a piquant political flavoring to the final year of preparations. Some officers of the association even feared that a pattern of political criteria might be set for future roundtables or world congresses—something that would effectively cripple IPSA. By the same token, bringing to Moscow from nonsocialist countries a thousand or more experts on politics presented the Soviet government with some unusual political risks and perhaps some opportunities.

Given the widespread attention before and after 1979 to the political nexus between congress and host country, we expected that respondents would virtually ignore other possible benefits accruing to the Soviet Union from its role as host country. Some of our questions about the functions of the Moscow world congress were nevertheless sufficiently open-ended to elicit a sense of the relative importance accorded economic, scientific, political, and other possible benefits. We also tackled the political issue directly. How important did the respondents regard political considerations to be in the selection of sites for ISCs? In particular, what were their views about the effects that hosting a political science congress by the USSR might have on Soviet domestic politics and on the international political environment? How important were these political considerations in determining the choices of individual political scientists to attend or not to attend the Moscow meeting? What did political scientists think about the utility of scientific sanctions, that is, limiting scientific communication and cooperation as a means to influence a target nation's foreign policy? Did they feel that the Soviet government had used the congress for propagandistic purposes and, if so, did these efforts inhibit scientific communication at the meeting? How much contact occurred between Eastern European scholars and their counterparts in the West? How did these contacts along with the experience of attending a meeting in the Soviet Union affect the participants' images of and attitudes toward the Soviet government and people?

This analysis of an ISC in which the political dimension was highly salient, namely, a political science congress in Moscow, should bring into sharper focus some of the political effects of all international scientific congresses, which are often obscured in the more homogeneous context of normal scientific discourse in Western countries. Important political consequences flow from the many decisions that are made concerning even the more technical aspects of any given ISC, such as forms of organization, operating procedures, and especially the choice of site. By virtue of their intellectual interest and expertise as political scientists, our respondents occupy a useful vantage point from which to consider the political factors that affect scientific communication at ISCs and the effects of this form of transnational activity on the international political environment.

Global Society

Our questionnaire did not specifically address the IPSA world congress's possible contribution to international science and world order. Indeed, we avoided questions we thought might elicit "idealistic" responses of the kneejerk variety. We nevertheless scrutinized the returned questionnaires, searching for views on two kinds of concerns. First, to what extent did the experience of political scientists who attended the IPSA congress in Moscow support the integrationist view of international scientific associations in general, that is, the view that they promote transnational values, peace, and justice? Second, and referring to the claims of dependency theorists, how much contact occurred between Third World scholars and political scientists from Western countries? Did the experience of the former at this particular meeting support the view that ISCs serve to reduce the knowledge and information gap between the developed and the developing countries?

Related to the first concern is a practical question: What impact did attendance have on the participants' images of and attitudes toward the Soviet Union, its people, and its scientific establishment? We would not expect a week's experience to produce far-reaching changes of a general nature; and even if they occurred, the social-psychological literature tells us, the passage of time would tend to diminish their effects. Marginal changes, such as making one's images more concrete through the addition of detail, were more likely. It was also likely that participants would obtain a much clearer notion of the interplay between politics and science in the Soviet Union. Those who had previously visited the Soviet Union or who occasionally, through their international activities, had dealt with Soviet scientists would, we anticipated, report encountering fewer surprises. Such findings are relevant to the broader question of whether or not ISCs contribute to the kinds of transnational interaction that promote peace.

Implications for Future IPSA World Congresses

Our analysis seeks not only to contribute to the study of international scientific associations as transnational actors but also to provide information of practical value to organizers of future international scientific congresses. What aspects of the congress itself facilitated or hindered scientific learning, for instance? Here we were interested not only in the participants' overall impressions of the congress, whether they found it satisfactory or not, but also in their views on its specific facets. A series of questions asked what they expected to find, for example, with respect to opportunities for informal interaction, and what they actually experienced. Further questions inquired what could be done to improve future IPSA congresses. Again we anticipated that the more professionally and internationally adept respondents would be those whose expectations and experiences were most closely matched.

Notes

1. The original members of the Preparatory Committee were Walter R. Sharp (United States), chair; John Goormaghtigh (Belgium), secretary; Raymond Aron (France); and William A. Robson (United Kingdom). They subsequently co-opted Angadipuram Appadorai (India) and Marcel Bridel (Switzerland). UNESCO's Third General Conference, held December 1948 in Beirut, authorized the director general to encourage the development of such international scientific associations.

2. Members of the provisional executive committee were Quincy Wright (United States), chair; Marcel Bridel (Switzerland) and Denis W. Brogan (United Kingdom), vice-chairs; and Jan Barents (Netherlands), Fethi Celikbas (Turkey), Maurice Duverger (France), Isaac Ganon (Uruguay), Elis W. Hastad (Sweden), H. Khosla (India), C. B. MacPherson (Canada), and Adam Schaff (Poland). The committee co-opted John Goormaghtigh (Belgium) as a member and François Goguel (France) as provisional executive secretary and treasurer. At the executive committee's meeting in February 1950, Jean Meynaud (France) was elected permanent executive secretary and treasurer (UNESCO, 1950b: 237); this title was changed in 1952 to secretary general and treasurer.

3. In almost all countries (excepting Canada, India, and the United States) it was necessary to organize a national association that could apply for IPSA membership. Those joining in 1950 were Israel, Poland, Sweden, and the United Kingdom; in 1951, Austria, Belgium, Greece, and Mexico; and in 1952, the Federal Republic of Germany, Finland, Italy, Yugoslavia, Japan, and Brazil (Philippart, 1970: 13).

4. Settling on a common terminology for the world congress has posed some minor problems. At the outset, program organizers identified themes, each with roundtables at which papers are presented and discussed. The terminology since at least the mid-1970s has focused on general *themes* (developed by consultants), broken down into a number of *sections* (organized by conveners), each of which typically has two *sessions* (presided over by chairs).

5. The papers and summaries of the discussions appear in UNESCO (1951).

6. For the Moscow congress, see Alker (1978), Bose (1978), Ludz (1979), Merle (1978), Semenov (1978), and Shakhnazarov (1978). Given the discipline's pluralism of subject matters and methodologies, of course, program organizers have not sought, nor could they effectively try, to police the structure of the individual sessions or the content of papers to ensure that they adhere to the stated themes.

7. Several of those listed on the program did not in fact appear in Moscow. Although the number of no-shows proved to be modestly disruptive and continues to be so, the problem may be intractable given current circumstances, namely, the need for funding and the weak mechanisms for social control enjoyed by international scientific associations.

8. In the late 1970s the Liberal government in Canada four times denied to the West German Marxist scholar, André Gunder Frank, visas to attend

conferences or give lectures (Scully, 1979). U.S. legislation dating from 1952 bans those "afflicted with psychopathic personality, or sexual deviation or a mental defect" from entering the country. Subsequent decisions by the Public Health Service to declassify homosexuality as a "mental disease or defect" (Treaster, 1979) and the Justice Department to turn back only those who openly declare their homosexuality (Pear, 1980) have modified the impact of the legislation, however, and courts are currently ascertaining its fundamental constitutionality.

In December 1985 the local organizing committee at Britain's University of Southampton, under pressure from the city council that would otherwise have withdrawn its financial support, voted to "disinvite" South Africans who planned to participate in the World Congress of Archeologists, scheduled for summer 1986. The International Union of Prehistoric and Protohistoric Scientists (IUPPS) accordingly cancelled its sponsorship and rescheduled the congress for summer 1987 in the West German city of Mainz. Southampton carried out its planned congress anyway, with as yet undetermined consequences for the IUPPS's future (Walker, 1986).

9. To secure the Israelis' visas in time for their scheduled departure for the Soviet Union, IPSA's secretary general, John E. Trent, had to fly first to Vienna to pick up the processed applications at the Soviet consulate and then to Israel to deliver them.

10. The question of civil rights violations in the Soviet Union became even more problematic for other scientific associations. In March 1979 some 2,400 American scientists pledged to suspend, as individuals, all professional cooperation with Soviet colleagues. The peak of organized political action came still later, with the mass campaign of the ad hoc organization, "Scientists for Sakharov, Orlov, and Sharansky" (SOS), which gathered signatures from 7,900 scientists and engineers from 44 countries on petitions pledging a six-month moratorium on scientific cooperation with Soviet scientists from May to November of 1980 (Seltzer, 1978; Stone and Spilhaus, 1980). The use of scientific cooperation as a lever to influence the domestic *and* foreign policies of the USSR gained momentum with the U.S. government's response to the Soviet invasion of Afghanistan. All official efforts at scientific cooperation under the intergovernmental agreements of 1972-1973 were suspended, and in an unprecedented action the National Academy of Sciences imposed a 6-month moratorium (subsequently extended for another 6 months) on all activities under its exchange program with the Soviet Academy of Sciences. As a result of these official and unofficial efforts to use scientific relations as a lever to influence Soviet behavior, symposia, visits, and even congresses were cancelled.

11. The executive committee also set up a standing "visa committee," charged with the task of investigating and reporting on complaints that a country hosting an IPSA meeting was violating the resolution's general principles. Guiding IPSA's (and, ultimately, APSA's) procedures was the memorandum offering "Advice to organizers of international scientific meetings," prepared by the International Council of Scientific Unions (ICSU, 1976). The most important correspondence and decisions on the proposed

boycott and conditions for holding the Moscow and future IPSA world congresses appear in the association's newsletter, *Participation*.

12. Several observers, such as the nationally syndicated columnist George F. Will (1978), found a delicious irony in the back-to-back decisions of APSA's general membership meeting to relocate the association's annual meeting of 1979 from Chicago (because the Illinois legislature had failed to ratify the Equal Rights Amendment) and not to boycott the IPSA world congress in Moscow.

13. To determine the extent to which respondents were willing to underline their own seriousness by attributing to others either frivolity or careerism, we asked them to distinguish the value of national meetings for themselves as against "other participants." Our expectations were that those who did not go to Moscow would be more apt to make such a distinction than those who did attend that congress, and that, among the latter group, respondents would attribute pretty much the same motives to others as to themselves.

14. The individual who is part of a closely knit research team may of course serve in a more representative capacity; our survey did not seek to ascertain the internal structure of research organizations.

THREE

Who Went to Moscow and Why?

Our survey of political scientists sought, first of all, to ascertain who participates in IPSA world congresses and why. Are they in effect a random sample of the international political science profession, or do they differ significantly from nonparticipants? To explore this point we questioned not only those who registered to attend the Moscow meetings in 1979 but also a control group of Canadian and U.S. political scientists who did not register. What general functions do respondents attribute to world congresses? To secure a baseline for evaluating such views, we initially asked respondents about the uses of national meetings. We then turned to the value of international meetings for individual scientists and other members of the political science consociation. Finally, we asked those who completed our questionnaire why they did or did not attend the IPSA world congress in Moscow.

Profile of Respondents

Registrants

Well over a thousand political scientists from 45 countries outside the socialist bloc registered to attend the IPSA world congress in Moscow. Not surprisingly, most of them are academics. Almost 9 in 10 (89%) indicated that their primary affiliation is with a university (with 75 percent of the entire sample holding a professorial title), while another 5 percent work for government agencies and 9 percent for private or governmental research organizations (multiple responses permitted). The median respondent, male (as are 87 percent of the registrants) and 41 years of age at the time of the Moscow meetings, embarked upon his or her professional career in 1967. By far the largest number (81%) finds research more interesting than teaching or administration.

The sample of registrants is also fairly accomplished in professional terms. Four in five (81%) hold a doctorate. Most (63%) with professorial duties enjoy the rank of full professor or equivalent; they constitute 49 percent of the entire sample of registrants. The registrants are active professionally: About half (49%) attend almost every annual meeting of their national political science association, and 69 percent say that they do so at least every other year. Well over half have published at least 3 books (62%) and 11 articles in scholarly journals (56%).

Finally, our registrants are oriented to international matters. As far as their main fields of research and teaching are concerned, 31 percent named international relations and another 27 percent comparative politics. Almost four in five (78%) speak at least one foreign language, half of them (40%) two or more. Four in five (80%) have attended at least one international scientific conference in addition to the IPSA meetings in Moscow; over half (54%) have attended five or more such conferences. Almost two-thirds (65%) have gone abroad at least once to conduct research and half (48%) at least twice.

Registrants vs. Nonregistrants

Is the degree of professionalism exhibited by those who signed up to go to Moscow in 1979 typical of the political science profession at large? To answer this question we may compare registrants from the United States and Canada ($n = 217$) with our control sample of political scientists from the same two countries who did not register to attend the Moscow meetings ($n = 238$). Before doing so, however, it should be noted that in most regards the North American registrants are quite similar in their professional characteristics to registrants from other regions. The two subsamples of registrants (those from North America and those from elsewhere) differ most markedly with respect to the latter's greater language skills and more frequent attendance at international scientific conferences.

Although the North American registrants and nonregistrants are roughly the same age, entered the profession at roughly the same point in their lives (at age 29 vs. 31), and are almost equally likely both to hold a doctorate (91 vs. 83 percent) and to work in an academic setting (91 vs. 81 percent), there the resemblance ends. The registrants are substantially more oriented to the political science profession than are those who did not attend the IPSA meetings in Moscow. In contrast to the three-quarters (74%) of the former who report attending at least every other annual meeting of the American or Canadian political science association (48 percent almost every year), only half (51%) of the nonregistrants do so (28 percent almost every year). Similarly, the former manifest greater interest in research than do the latter (77 vs. 55 percent). They have also been more productive: The median registrant reports having published 3 or 4 books and 11 to 20 scholarly articles, the median nonregistrant 1 or 2 books and 3 or 4 articles. Not surprisingly, in view of such behavior, the registrants enjoy higher academic status. Three in five of them (58%), as opposed to only a quarter of the nonregistrants (23%), are full professors.

Then, too, registrants have a greater range of international research skills and experience than do nonregistrants. They are more likely to be bi- or multilingual: Three in five registrants (62%) speak at least one foreign language (23 percent two or more), while only two in five nonregistrants (42%) do so (14 percent two or more). Three in five nonregistrants report never having attended an international scientific conference (59%) or taken a research trip abroad (60%). In contrast, about half that many registrants indicated that they had attended no more than one such conference (27%) and that they had no overseas research experience (31%).

These data suggest that our main sample of 420 political scientists who registered to attend the IPSA meetings in Moscow is far from typical of the profession as a whole. We are dealing with a special group of scholars—individuals who have been unusually productive, have advanced in their scholarly careers, and are active internationally as well as in their national associations. And yet there are differences even among them.

Professionalism and Internationalism

To highlight these differences more than the above profile can, we developed five simple scales to characterize the respondents: professional activity, professional status, international research competence, international activity, and experience in world congresses organized by IPSA. To some slight degree a couple of the scales overlap, but each by itself points to a significant dimension that may help to explain respondents' views on international scientific conferences in general and the IPSA congress in Moscow in particular. (Note: All scales, standardized to range from 0 to 10 points, are additive; for details, see Appendix C.)

Professional activity. Political scientists who are professionally active are likely to take a view quite different from that of the less active. Our scale of professional activity looked at the respondent's position on five questions: attendance at annual meetings of the respondent's national political science association; orientation to research; published books and monographs; scientific articles; and recent publications record. To score the maximum of 10 points on this scale the respondent would have to attend annual meetings almost every year, be strongly interested in research, and have published at least 5 books and 21 articles, 6 or more of them in the past 2 years.

Table 3.1 shows how the various categories of registrants and nonregistrants scored on the scale of professional activity and other scales. The main difference to be noted is between the two primary samples: The average scores for all registrants (5.9) and North American registrants (5.8) are well over two points higher than the score of our control sample of North American nonregistrants (3.6). Political scientists from Western countries other than the United States and Canada turned out to be the most active professionally, while Third World scholars scored slightly higher than North Americans. (Mean scores for nonregistrants are, for instructors in U.S. graduate departments, 4.2; CPSA members, 4.0; and APSA members, 3.4.)

Professional status. Among the many indicators of professional standing or status are academic accomplishments, title and position, and length of time in the profession. The person scoring 10 points on this scale would have a doctorate, be a full professor or director of a research institute or the equivalent, have been professionally active for more than 20 years, and be the author of 5 or more books and at least 21 scholarly articles.

Again we see an important difference between those who registered to attend the IPSA meetings in Moscow and those who did not. In this case, however, North Americans are highest on the totem pole of professional standing, and the category of other Westerners lowest. North American registrants enjoy a status two full points higher than their compatriots who did not sign up for the congress. (The mean score for nonregistering instructors in U.S. graduate departments is 5.2, that for CPSA and APSA members 4.1.)

International research competence. The ability to communicate and perform research in foreign languages and actual experience conducting research abroad are frequently touted as skills predisposing scholars to take part in international scientific activities and rendering them more able to make sophisticated judgments about the quality of such activities. The person judged in this survey to be most highly capable of conducting international research can communicate effectively in at least two foreign languages, actually uses a foreign language in his or her research, and has gone abroad at least three times for research purposes.

North Americans lag considerably behind political scientists from other parts of the world in their linguistic skills and overseas research experience. Respondents from the United States, with a mean score of 5.1, are in this respect substantially below Canadians, who have a mean score of 6.1. Even so, registrants from these two countries rank considerably higher than the

Table 3.1 Variations in Professionalism and Internationalism
Mean Scores Standardized on an Eleven-Point Scale[a]

	Registrants				Non-registrants
Scale	North American	Other Western	Third World	Total	
Professional activity	5.8	6.0	5.8	5.9	3.6
Professional status	6.3	5.7	5.8	6.0	4.3
International research competence	5.3	6.8	6.1	5.9	2.2
International activity	5.2	5.6	5.2	5.3	2.7
IPSA experience	1.9	2.2	0.7	1.9	0.3

[a]The original (additive) scales ranged from 6 points (0-5) to 11 points (0-10); see Appendix C for details.

comparable sample of nonregistrants (among whom CPSA members average 4.2 points, instructors in U.S. graduate departments of political science 2.5 points, and the general APSA membership 1.9 points). The most internationally competent researchers, according to these data, are from that complex of countries including Western Europe, Australia, and Israel (6.8 points).

International activity. The questionnaire includes several items designed to ascertain the extent to which respondents actively participate in international research. Do they focus their attention on foreign countries or international relations? Do they conduct research in foreign settings or meet together with foreign scholars? A political scientist scoring the maximum on this scale would have attended at least six international scientific conferences both at home and abroad, made three or more overseas research trips, specialized in either international relations or comparative politics, and given a global focus to his or her teaching and research.

Political scientists from Western countries outside North America once again emerge as the most international-minded. The gap between them and both North Americans and registrants from the Third World is nonetheless not great. The fact that Canadians score higher (mean score = 5.7) than U.S. respondents (mean score = 5.0) is doubtless attributable to the significance for political scientists throughout North America of both APSA meetings and research institutions and libraries in the United States. The difference between North American registrants and nonregistrants (a gap of 2.5 points) is more remarkable. (Canadian nonregistrants, with a mean score of 3.6 points, also manifest more international research activity than either instructors in U.S. graduate departments or APSA members, who score 2.7 and 2.5 points, respectively.)

IPSA experience. Still another way to characterize our respondents is according to the number of IPSA world congresses they attended before the meetings held in 1979 in Moscow. We asked about participation in previous triennial world congresses held in Geneva (1964), Brussels (1967), Munich (1970), Montréal (1973), and Edinburgh (1976). Respondents scored two points for each of these meetings they had attended.

Only 2 percent of the registrants faithfully attended all IPSA world congresses since 1964. West Europeans were more likely to have attended three or more of them than were North Americans—an observation that is not very surprising in view of the fact that four of these five meetings took place in Europe. Similarly, Canadians, who had the opportunity to attend the IPSA world congress of 1973 in Montréal, have a higher mean score than do their intellectual companions south of the border (2.5 as opposed to 1.7 points). Political scientists from the Third World are by and large newcomers to IPSA activities. As far as the difference between North American registrants and nonregistrants is concerned, it is apparent that a readiness to go to Moscow in 1979 went hand in hand with previous experience with IPSA world congresses. Among the nonregistrants, too, Canadians were more likely to have attended an IPSA world congress (mean score = 1.0) than were political scientists in the United States (mean scores of 0.3 for APSA members and 0.1 for instructors in graduate departments).

Intercorrelations among scores. Each of the five scales is positively correlated with the others (Table 3.2). This means that the more professionally active an individual is, the more likely that individual is to enjoy a high professional standing, be active internationally, have attended previous IPSA world congresses, and so forth. In only a couple of cases, however, are the correlation coefficients sufficiently high to warrant special attention. The first is between professional status and level of professional activity, where the two variables account for two-fifths of the variance in the data ($r = .63$; $r^2 = .40$). Thus, if we know how active a person is in the political science profession, we can, very roughly speaking, predict two out of five times how that individual scores on our scale of professional status. Second, levels of international competence and international activity are highly correlated ($r = .61$; $r^2 = .38$). It is also interesting to note that the higher an individual's professional status and the more active professionally that individual is, the more likely he or she is to have attended past IPSA world congresses.

What all these data indicate is that the political scientists who registered to attend the IPSA world congress in Moscow (those to whom we shall devote most of our attention) constitute a highly select group. Professionally, they are more active at home and abroad than their fellow scholars who planned to stay at home in 1979; and, internationally, they

Table 3.2 Intercorrelation of Scores on Scales[a]

	Professional Activity	Professional Status	International Competence	International Activity
Professional Status	.63			
International Competence	.17	.20		
International Activity	.29	.31	.61	
IPSA Experience	.35	.39	.23	.32

[a] Pearson's r; all coefficients are significant at the $p < .001$ level.

possess greater experience and skills for research. While the data show that high professional status is associated with attendance at IPSA congresses, they cannot tell us whether or not any country's leading political scientists, that is, those recognized as key disciplinary leaders, are the ones participating in these meetings. We may nevertheless reasonably conclude that our registrants represent the *leading stratum* of political scientists in North America and probably across the world.

Why Attend Professional Meetings?

Professional meetings are a standard component of contemporary scientific disciplines. By now, most national political science associations throughout the world hold annual or less frequent general meetings at which members read and discuss papers and transact the association's business. In large countries, such as the United States, there may be regional and even state associations, each organizing its own annual convention. Ever more subdisciplinary groups also hold regular meetings for specialists. Some of these conclaves take place over the course of several days and involve thousands of participants, while others are more modest in both respects.

The political scientists we questioned attend such meetings fairly regularly. Among those who registered for the IPSA meetings in Moscow, and whose national associations hold annual meetings, almost three-quarters indicate that they participate in the latter almost every year (51%) or approximately every other year (23%); only 7 percent report never doing so. Nonregistrants in North America were also asked about attending regional and subdisciplinary as well as national meetings (see Appendix B). About half (51%) attend APSA or CPSA meetings regularly, that is, approximately every other year or more frequently, and somewhat fewer regularly go to conventions of regional associations (45%) or subdisciplinary groups (42%).

(The numbers never attending amount to 13 percent for APSA/CPSA, 27 percent for regional, and 34 percent for subdisciplinary meetings.)

Well over half of the respondents see the main functions of these disciplinary meetings to be scientific (Table 3.3). The meetings are useful, they say, primarily for general communication and professional contacts, and also for learning something new. Personal goals such as seeing old friends and career development definitely take second place. Only the occasional individual mentions the value of subdisciplinary meetings for institution-building in the specialized fields. The distributions of responses are quite consistent across the various categories of respondents and conferences (with correlation coefficients, all highly significant statistically, ranging from .85 to .96).[1] Moreover, the respondents assert that these various meetings serve the same hierarchy of functions for most other participants as for themselves.[2]

Some distinctions among responses are nevertheless noticeable. North American political scientists who did not register to attend the Moscow world congress emphasize the scientific value of subdisciplinary meetings more than national and regional ones. They are also more apt to downgrade the importance of the meetings as far as they themselves are concerned (11 percent for each of the three kinds of meetings) than with respect to others (2-3%), and to attribute careerist motives to others (averaging 22 percent) rather than to themselves (averaging 12 percent). North American registrants are more oriented to the scientific functions of national meetings than are nonregistrants (68 to 58 percent, respectively)—but here it must be added that the registrants from outside North America are even more so (80%).[3]

These modest differences aside, a picture emerges of political scientists who are reasonably well tied into their national associations, as indicated by attendance at annual meetings, and who stress the scientific function of these meetings. Somewhat fewer of the North American registrants participate in regional or subdisciplinary meetings (even though they recognize the latter as being of more scientific value than either national or regional meetings).

Value of International Scientific Congresses

When it comes to international as opposed to national disciplinary meetings, political scientists see a more differentiated variety of functions being performed. Our questionnaires asked respondents to indicate what they considered to be the main functions of international conferences for (1) the individual participant, (2) the political science profession as a whole, and (3) the host country. The questionnaires went on to ask which of all these functions respondents think is the single chief value of international scientific congresses in the field of political science. This section reports the

Table 3.3 Perceived Value to Self of National, Regional, and Subdisciplinary Meetings
Views of North American Registrants and Nonregistrants

	Registrants		Nonregistrants					
	National		National		Regional		Subdisc.	
	N	%	N	%	N	%	N	%
Scientific								
General communication	76	21	55	20	35	15	51	25
Contacts	86	23	55	20	50	22	36	17
New information	80	22	38	14	38	17	36	17
Other	9	2	7	3	5	2	9	4
Total	251	68	155	58	128	56	132	64
Political								
Personal	–	–	–	–	–	–	–	–
Career development	39	11	33	12	30	13	22	11
Social; see friends	58	16	46	17	41	18	24	12
Travel	2	1	5	2	5	2	4	2
Total	99	27	84	31	76	33	50	24
Disciplinary	–	–	–	–	–	–	2	1
Other	–	–	–	–	–	–	–	–
Little or no value	19	5	30	11	25	11	23	11
No response	22	*	88	*	106	*	124	*
Total[a]	391	100	357	100	335	100	331	100

[a]Multiple responses recorded. Because of rounding, percentage columns (which omit "no response" category) may not add to 100 percent.

responses as they relate to *all three* categories of actors. We shall leave to Chapter 4, however, a more detailed consideration of ISCs' scientific impact on individual scientists, and to Chapter 5 the functions of ISCs for the host country.

Before exploring the perceived functionality of ISCs for individual scientists, the discipline, and the host country, we should note two areas of general interest. The first pertains to the distinction between registrants and nonregistrants (Table 3.4). The overall distribution of responses to the question about an ISC's chief function shows no statistically significant difference between those who had and those who had not registered to attend the IPSA world congress in Moscow.[4] Indeed, virtually the only point worth noting is the registrant's secondary concentration on its scientific value for the host country, while the nonregistrants split their secondary concentration

Table 3.4 Chief Functions of International Scientific Congresses in Political Science

	For the Individual		For the Profession		For the Host Country		Overall Chief Value	
	N	%	N	%	N	%	N	%
Scientific								
Registrants	589	86	360	63	123	22	243	69
Nonregistrants	247	81	150	65	20	10	125	76
Total	836	84	510	64	143	19	368	73
Political								
Registrants	1	0	12	2	413	74	13	4
Nonregistrants	4	1	3	1	149	73	2	1
Total	5	1	15	2	562	74	15	3
Personal								
Registrants	97	14	22	4	-	-	6	2
Nonregistrants	53	17	14	6	-	-	8	5
Total	150	15	36	4	-	-	14	3
Disciplinary								
Registrants	-	-	167	29	-	-	85	24
Nonregistrants	-	-	58	25	23	11	23	14
Total	-	-	225	28	23	3	108	21
Other								
Registrants	1	0	2	0	2	0	3	1
Nonregistrants	-	-	1	0	-	-	-	-
Total	1	0	3	0	2	0	3	1
Little or no value								
Registrants	-	-	6	1	18	3	3	1
Nonregistrants	1	0	6	3	11	5	6	4
Total	1	0	12	1	29	4	9	2
No response								
Registrants	13	*	26	*	57	*	67	*
Nonregistrants	58	*	73	*	98	*	74	*
Total	71	*	99	*	155	*	141	*
Total[a]								
Registrants	701	100	595	100	613	100	420	100
Nonregistrants	363	100	305	100	301	100	238	100
Total	1064	100	900	100	914	100	658	100

[a]Multiple responses recorded. Because of rounding, percentage columns (which omit "no response" category) may not add to 100 percent.

between the ISC's scientific and disciplinary value for the host country. This may nevertheless be a distinction without a difference: Response categories for the former category emphasized political science in the host country, while those for the latter stressed political science as an international discipline. Table 3.5 breaks down into finer subcategories the registrants' responses.

A second general question asked respondents how important they considered the functions they mentioned to be for the individual, profession, and host country (Table 3.6). Here, as in the case of the functions named, nonregistrants are less apt than registrants to respond, but, when they do, they also express a less positive orientation toward the overall value of international political science congresses.

Value of ISCs for the Individual

Our respondents make quite clear their view that the individual will gain most from these congresses' scientific aspects. In fact, 86 percent of those who went or had planned to go to the IPSA meetings in Moscow and 81 percent of the nonregistrants cite such values (Table 3.4). These include

- professional contacts (29% of the two samples together)[5]
- general communication (21%)
- broadened international perspectives (16%)
- acquisition of information about the field's new literature, approaches, and research techniques (17%).

Registrants display a much more specific orientation than nonregistrants (Table 3.5). They place the greatest weight on the contacts one is likely to make on such occasions, while those who did not register for the Moscow meetings look more at an expected broadening of international perspectives. Personal gain weighs far less heavily in their minds than scientific values (14 percent for registrants, 17 percent for nonregistrants):

- career development (8%)
- travel and tourism (5%)
- social activities or seeing friends (2%).

Finally, neither set of respondents is much taken by the prospects for political advantages to be gained through these meetings; and no one mentions disciplinary values that could be served.

Are these functions important for the individual participant? Registrants definitely think so and nonregistrants are only a bit more doubtful (Table 3.6). Almost two-thirds of the former group answering the question indicate that the functions served are very important and about half that number

Table 3.5 Registrants' Views on Functions of International Political Science Congresses

	For the Individual N	For the Individual %	For the Profession N	For the Profession %	For the Host country N	For the Host country %	Overall Chief Value N	Overall Chief Value %
Scientific								
General communication	150	22	172	30	49	9	124	35
New information	86	13	23	4	-	-	10	3
Broaden perspectives: gen'l	29	4	14	2	-	-	9	3
Broaden perspectives: int'l	86	13	47	8	12	2	49	14
Contacts	223	32	67	12	50	9	48	14
Facilitate collab./research	15	2	37	7	12	2	3	1
Total	589	86	360	63	123	22	243	69
Political								
International	1	0	12	2	-	-	13	4
National: image; prestige	-	-	-	-	178	32	-	-
National: economic	-	-	-	-	49	9	-	-
National: scientific	-	-	-	-	72	13	-	-
National: other	-	-	-	-	31	6	-	-
National: varies by country	-	-	-	-	83	15	-	-
Total	1	0	12	2	413	74	13	4
Personal								
Career development	57	8	17	3	-	-	4	1
Social; travel	40	6	5	1	-	-	2	1
Total	97	14	22	4	-	-	6	2
Disciplinary								
Prestige; disc. development	-	-	60	11	-	-	12	3
Improve pol. sci. knowledge	-	-	49	9	-	-	17	5
Build int'l discipline	-	-	58	10	-	-	56	16
Total	-	-	167	29	-	-	85	24
Other	1	0	2	0	2	0	3	1
Little or no value	-	-	6	1	18	3	3	1
No response	13	*	26	*	57	*	67	*
Total[a]	701	100	595	100	613	100	420	100

[a]Multiple responses recorded. Because of rounding, percentage columns (which omit "no response" category) may not add to 100 percent.

Table 3.6 Importance of International Political Science Congresses

	Registrants		Non-registrants		All Respondents	
	N	%	N	%	N	%
For the individual participant						
Very important	251	65	67	36	318	55
Somewhat important	126	32	96	51	222	39
Not very important	10	3	17	9	27	5
Not at all important	1	0	8	4	9	2
Varies or no response	32	*	50	*	82	*
Total[a]	420	100	238	100	658	100
Average score[b]	2.62		2.18		2.47	
For the political science profession						
Very important	199	52	66	36	265	46
Somewhat important	159	41	82	44	241	42
Not very important	21	5	27	15	48	8
Not at all important	7	2	10	5	17	3
Varies or no response	34	*	53	*	87	*
Total[a]	420	100	238	100	658	100
Average score[b]	2.42		2.10		2.32	
For the host country						
Very important	79	22	33	19	112	21
Somewhat important	143	40	59	35	202	38
Not very important	106	30	62	36	168	32
Not at all important	31	9	17	10	48	9
Varies or no response	61	*	67	*	128	*
Total[a]	420	100	238	100	658	100
Average score[b]	1.75		1.63		1.71	

[a] "Importance varies" and "no response" categories are not included in calculations for either percentage distributions or average scores. Because of rounding, columns may not add to 100 percent.
[b] Average scores are computed according to the following weights: Very important = 3; somewhat important = 2; not very important = 1; and not at all important = 0.

considers them somewhat important. The median response for nonregistrants is "somewhat important." Even among those who did not go to Moscow, then, seven in eight think these kinds of meetings are at least somewhat important.

Value of ISCs for the Profession

Disciplinary values are viewed as more important for the profession than for the individual. Asked what function international congresses play for the political science profession, almost two-thirds (64%) of the responses given by our combined samples mention scientific values such as those discussed above, but another 28 percent point to disciplinary values (and barely 1 percent indicates that international congresses have little or no value for political science as a discipline). Three disciplinary themes are dominant in these responses.

One focuses on developing the prestige and identity of the political science profession (10 percent of the combined sample). The mere fact that such international congresses are held gives the profession a cachet of prestige and, over the long run, a more deeply held sense of the profession's legitimacy as a scientific discipline. Similarly, bringing together scholars from different countries can enhance their awareness of the degree to which they share similar interests and approaches, or will at least be able to deal with alternative ones within a broad, common framework. Thus, congresses serve a latent integrative function[6] by enhancing political scientists' sense of community and professional identity.

A second theme emphasizes the role of international congresses in internationalizing political science (10%). Many respondents suggest that the "cross-fertilization of ideas" across national boundaries—a phrase that frequently appears on completed questionnaires—helps to identify transnational research problems and stimulates new lines of research. International congresses provide an opportunity to test the applicability across political systems of theories, findings, and conclusions, and facilitate the dissemination of new methodologies and bodies of data.[7] Other respondents point to more logistical and practical functions, such as facilitating the development of transnational study groups and international collaboration.

Third, a few responses (8%) stress the part played by international congresses in keeping the science in political science. "Tunnel vision" and ideological and cultural "blinders" are some of the metaphors used to convey what some respondents see to be unfortunate tendencies toward parochialism or ethnocentricity in political science, when assumptions and conclusions are not subjected to the challenges and criticisms of scholarly exchange in an international context. Others refer to the value of international congresses for improving the study of political science—its methods and substantive identity as a discipline.

Respondents are somewhat less confident that the functions international political science congresses serve for the profession are as important as those they serve for individual participants (Table 3.6). Again, nonregistrants express greater doubts than those who actually paid their money to register for the Moscow meetings.

Value of ISCs for the Host Country

International political science congresses are seen as being even less important for the host country. The median response of both registrants and nonregistrants to our question on this point is that the congresses are "somewhat important." Moreover, over two-fifths of the entire sample describe the functions served for the host country as not very or not at all important—and those closest to such congresses, that is, those who registered for the Moscow meetings, are not much more likely to term those functions important than are the nonregistrants.

Asked what functions the congresses serve for the host country, more than three in five (61 percent of the entire sample) respond in terms that have little to do with science. The most popular response (37%) stresses national prestige, public relations, or some variation on this theme. A point that merits attention here, although it will be discussed in greater detail in Chapter 5, is that only a very small number (6%) feel that the IPSA world congress gave the Soviet Union greater legitimacy in the eyes of the world, opportunities for propaganda, or some other political advantage. Far more important in this category of response is the perceived likelihood that foreign scholars would increase their knowledge and understanding of the country. About 1 in 11 (9%) cites economic advantages, most notably receipts from tourism. Another one in seven (14%) indicates that such domestic gains vary with the country hosting the congress, and roughly a third of these respondents note that the Soviet Union would gain advantages that other countries would not.

Most of the remainder—only 4 percent see little or no value accruing to the host country—point to expectable scientific gains. The largest number of these (19%) refer to the intellectual stimulation that international congresses provide for local political scientists, as well as opportunities to communicate with foreign scholars and to participate more actively in the profession. Some suggest that this improved communication and participation can encourage and improve indigenous research in political science. A few others (3%), all of them respondents who had not registered to attend the Moscow meetings, argue concomitantly that the organizational experience obtained by political scientists in the host country will assist the profession as a whole. A substantial number of respondents (13%) also notes that the increased visibility and prestige, both domestic and international, that an international congress provides political scientists in the host country enhances the status of their professional association.[8]

Chief Value of International Scientific Congresses

Not surprisingly, given the respondents' views on the value of international congresses for the individual scientist and profession, when they turn to identifying the single chief value (Table 3.4) they concentrate on the congresses' scientific contributions. One in three (34%) mentions general scientific communication, almost that many reducing parochialism either among individual scientists (18%) or in the discipline as a whole (13%), and a quarter mentions methods other aspects of the scientific process such as building contacts (13%) and enhancing knowledge or general perspectives (10%). Those registered to attend the Moscow meetings are almost twice as likely as nonregistrants to emphasize disciplinary values, while the latter focus more than the former on the scientific goal of broadening international perspectives.

Looking solely at registrants, we find remarkably few differences among the categories of respondents. Political scientists from North America, other Western countries, and the Third World are fairly well agreed on the chief purposes of international congresses in their field. North Americans are slightly more apt to identify disciplinary purposes and other Westerners scientific purposes, but the distinctions are not significant statistically.[9] The same conclusion emerges when we divide the registrants according to whether they are high or low in terms of professional activity, professional status, international activity, international competence, or IPSA experience. The relative importance of the various types of purposes is a very robust finding.[10]

In sum, political scientists believe that international congresses serve a variety of purposes: primarily scientific for the individual, scientific and organizational for the political science discipline, and primarily political for the host country. Differences between North American registrants for the Moscow meetings and nonregistrants are discernible but are not statistically significant. Nor does it matter much where the registrants live and work, or how active they are in the profession. The respondents consider the various purposes they identify to be important—more so, as we shall see later, for the individual and discipline than for the host country. It is the political scientist and the political science profession as a whole that benefit from international congresses. To the extent that a country stands to gain from hosting a congress, the gain is marginal rather than significant.

Deciding to Go to Moscow

Ultimately, however political scientists view the functionality of a particular ISC for themselves and others, they must decide whether or not to attend. This section examines the reasons given by those who registered and attended the IPSA world congress of 1979, those who registered but did not attend it, and those North Americans who did not sign up to go to Moscow.

Participants

Those who went to Moscow in 1979 say they did so primarily for either scientific or personal reasons. The most prominent explanations offered by those who attended for scientific reasons were contacts (14%), broadened international perspectives (11%), and general communication (10%). The predominant personal reason, career development, which accounts for 28 percent of the responses, centers on practical considerations such as the fact that the respondent was invited to present a paper or otherwise participate in the program. If we consider such responses as being related to the scientific enterprise, then we might conclude that close to three in four (73%) were seeking to develop further their skills as political scientists. About a quarter of that number (19%), however, simply cites the desire to visit Moscow or travel in the Soviet Union. (North Americans are a bit more likely than others to give this last response, but they are also more likely to say that they went to broaden their perspectives and learn about the Soviet system.) As we shall see in Chapter 5, political reasons did not play a significant role in participants' decisions on this matter.

A further question about which of the reasons given is the primary one elicited roughly the same distribution of responses: 41 percent scientific, 33 percent career development (again, essentially, the chance to participate in the program), 17 percent travel and tourism, and only a handful political.

Non-Attending Registrants

Fifty of those responding to our questionnaire registered but ultimately did not go to Moscow. Why? The main reasons they cite are personal. Over half (55%) refer to what might be called reasons of convenience—family obligations, illness, or the like—and another quarter (24%) to the dearth of financial resources. Only five of these responses (8%) mention problems of scientific communication and another six (10%) political restrictions in the Soviet Union. The subsequent question about the primary reason produced an almost identical set of responses (with personal reasons climbing to a total of 85 percent).

Nonregistrants

The sample of political scientists in Canada and the United States who did not register to attend the Moscow meetings also stresses personal considerations behind their individual decisions. The most prominent one is the lack of funds (41%), but lack of time or interest also played an important role (33%). Another set of respondents was either unaware of the meetings or had not been invited to attend them (6 percent each). Five and eight percent, respectively, refer to anticipated difficulties of scientific communication and political considerations. Respondents from the United States are somewhat more likely to mention political considerations (9%) than are Canadians (5%), who in turn are slightly more concerned about scientific communication, but both groups clearly identify the lack of funding, time, or interest as the main thing keeping them away from Moscow.

The data on reasons for attending or not attending the Moscow meetings are fairly unambiguous. Those who went did so mainly because they expected to learn something or develop their professional capabilities. A much smaller proportion saw the meetings primarily as an opportunity to visit a part of the world otherwise less easily accessible to them. It was not politics but mostly practical considerations that kept the rest at home.

Notes

1. The coefficients are: for national vs. regional meetings, $r = .96$, $p < .001$; national vs. subdisciplinary meetings, $r = .93$, $p < .001$; regional vs. subdisciplinary meetings, $r = .85$, $p < .01$; and for nonregistrants vs. North American registrants, $r = .90$, $p < .01$.

2. The coefficients for perceived value to self vs. others are: among registrants, for national meetings, $r = .82$, $p < .01$; regional meetings, $r = .83$, $p < .01$; subdisciplinary meetings, $r = .90$, $p < .001$; and, among all registrants, for national meetings, $r = .96$, $p < .001$.

3. Even so, the distribution of responses of North American vs. other registrants is remarkably similar, with $r = .87$, $p < .001$.

4. The correlation coefficients for the distribution of responses by registrants vs. nonregistrants are: function for the individual, $r = .87$, $p < .001$; the profession, $r = .77$, $p < .01$; host country, $r = .87$, $p < .001$; and chief value, $r = .88$, $p < .001$.

5. Although the desire to establish and maintain contacts could be construed as a career-related benefit, most of those who used the word "contacts" placed it in the broader context of scholarly exchange.

6. "Latent functions," in Merton's (1957: 51) terminology, refer to observable objective "consequences which are neither intended nor recognized." We shall return to this point in Chapter 6.

7. See Nuttin's (1974: 299) comment: "The main purpose . . . of

symposia in general international congresses should be a constructive 'confrontation' of approaches, and a comparison of theoretical points of view, in an effort to learn from each other and to escape from the narrow circle of problems and methods in which research in some countries is often confined for several years."

8. This finding corresponds with Archie Brown's (1984: 322-323) argument, cited earlier, that holding the IPSA world congress in Moscow provided "a considerable stimulus to the development of political science in the USSR."

9. The correlation coefficients by region are: for North American vs. other Western respondents, $r = .87$; North American vs. Third World respondents, $r = .85$; and other Western vs. Third World respondents, $r = .92$—all significant at the level of $p < .001$.

10. Dividing each distribution into equal halves, the correlation coefficients for the top vs. bottom halves are: for professional activity (0-6.4 vs. 6.5-10), $r = .96$; professional status (0-6.9 vs. 7-10), $r = .98$; international activity (0-6.1 vs. 6.2-10), $r = .99$; international competence (0-6.9 vs. 7-10), $r = .96$; and IPSA experience (0-1.4 vs. 1.5-10), $r = .97$. All these coefficients are significant at the level of $p < .001$.

FOUR
An Occasion for Learning

Although international scientific congresses are perceived as serving a variety of purposes, scientific communication remains the primary reason given to justify the expenditure of time and resources required to organize and participate in such meetings. This chapter investigates the validity of such claims. It addresses four kinds of questions. Two concern short-term learning. First, how do participants in IPSA's world congress in Moscow assess it as a context for scientific exchange? How did their experiences match up with their expectations before they went to the Soviet Union? Second, turning to a general area where learning seemed possible, we sought to determine what impact attending the conference had on images of and attitudes toward the Soviet Union and its people. Do IPSA members feel they gained a better understanding of life and scholarship in the Soviet Union?

The other pair of questions concerns the congress's effect on the participants' long-term environment for learning. Third, how did the experience of having attended the conference change their network of colleagues and interaction with them? Finally, in what ways did participation in the congress change the respondents' scholarship or other professional activities? Since some of our questions on these points stem from a survey conducted by the Johns Hopkins Center for Research in Scientific Communication of participants in the international congresses of psychology and sociology, both held in 1966, comparative data about the variable impact of international scientific congresses across time and disciplines enriches our findings.

It is worth reminding ourselves as we examine the data that, since the survey was conducted a good year after the end of the IPSA meetings in Moscow, we are dealing with recalled experiences. It would have been preferable to have sent out before-and-after questionnaires to tap changes in perceptions that might be attributed directly to the impact of the world congress, for we know that subsequent events affect the ways in which we recall the thoughts we had before those events occurred. Recalled experiences may nevertheless provide us with insights into the long-range effect of attending international conferences.

Expectations and Experiences

"What we anticipate seldom occurs," Benjamin Disraeli wrote in his novel, *Henrietta Temple*. And yet social psychologists have frequently pointed out that our expectations about a social setting can set up a chain of self-fulfilling prophecies, and that, once we commit ourselves to an image of what will occur, we are quite apt to "see" that outcome irrespective of the objective situation. For almost three-quarters of our respondents, the visit to the IPSA world congress in Moscow was their first in the Soviet Union. Given the facts that most students of political science have a keen awareness of the international political arena and that much has been written about Soviet life and behavior, it would be surprising indeed if our respondents did not undertake their visit with some sharply defined expectations about what they would encounter. What were some of these expectations? Was the reality they encountered anything like what the respondents expected?

To find out more about this dimension of conference outcomes, we gave respondents a series of 11 statements, and asked them 2 questions about each. As an example, one assertion was: "I would have a great deal of contact with Soviet scholars at the congress." The first question queried the extent to which the statement corresponded with the respondents' *expectations* about what they would encounter in the Soviet Union. Possible responses were "not at all what I expected," "only a little like I expected," "approximately what I expected," or "exactly what I expected." The second question inquired how closely the assertion in fact described what the respondent *experienced* in the Soviet Union. Here the response categories were "not at all what actually happened," "only a little like what happened," "approximately what happened," and "exactly what happened." In each case we assigned scores across the range of categories from 1 (= "not at all what I expected/what happened") to 4 (= "exactly what I expected/what happened"). The sample's mean expectation about contact with Soviet scholars (2.37) was between the categories "somewhat" and "approximately what I expected." The mean experience reported (2.48) was slightly above the anticipated condition.

For the sake of convenience we may group the eleven statements into four areas as follows:

Contact with East Europeans

  b. I would have little social contact with people in the USSR (other than Congress participants). (Note: In the analysis the scores for this question have been reversed to make the question more similar to the following two.)
  c. I would have a great deal of contact with Soviet scholars at the Congress.
  d. I would have a great deal of contact with other East European scholars at the Congress.

Professional Learning

  f. A substantial number of Congress participants would have research interests similar to my own.
  g. I would learn something professionally useful from papers and comments presented in the formal sessions by Soviet and East European participants.
  j. There would be opportunities for informal interaction with Congress participants from other countries that would contribute to my ongoing and future research.

Organization to Permit Interaction

  e. The organization of the Congress itself would facilitate interaction among participants.
  h. Participants in formal sessions would be able to raise any topics and present any points of view they wished (even on highly contentious "cold war" issues).
  i. The procedures followed by panel chairpersons would encourage uninhibited discussion and the presentation of a wide range of viewpoints.

General

  a. The accommodations (including hotel and provision for meals) would be adequate to my needs.
  k. Overall, my visit to the IPSA World Congress in Moscow would be a satisfying personal experience.

Table 4.1 arranges the four groupings in order of ascending expectations.

Table 4.1 Expectations and Experiences: Mean Scores

Statement	Expectation	Experience	Difference	Individual Corr.Coeff.
East European contacts				
b. Soviet people	1.97	2.09	+.12	.51***
c. Soviet scholars	2.37	2.48	+.11	.14**
d. East European scholars	2.45	2.59	+.14	.33***
Average	2.26	2.39	+.13	
Professional learning				
f. Partic. interests similar	2.55	2.81	+.26	.51***
g. Soviet/E.Eur. contribution	2.43	2.55	+.12	.31***
j. Informal interaction	3.04	2.87	−.18	.47***
Average	2.67	2.74	+.07	
Organization				
e. Facilitate interaction	2.72	2.55	−.17	.42***
h. Free discussion	2.74	2.70	−.04	.42***
i. Chairs facilitate disc.	2.77	2.66	−.11	.34***
Average	2.74	2.64	−.11	
General				
a. Accommodations adequate	2.99	3.03	+.04	.50***
k. Satisfying experience	3.30	3.32	+.02	.54***
Average	3.15	3.18	+.03	—
Overall averages	2.67	2.70	+.03	.41

Significance levels: ** = $p < .01$; *** = $p < .001$.

Thus respondents report having been far more confident that their general experiences at the congress would be positive (mean score of 3.30) than that they would have adequate opportunities to interact significantly with Soviet and East European scholars and citizens (mean score of 1.97).

What respondents experienced was not far removed from what they had anticipated. (A Pearsonian product-moment correlation for the mean scores of expectations and experiences shows much overall consistency: $r = .93, p < .001$.) Respondents were most pleasantly surprised (difference, or $d = +.26$) by encountering scholars with interests similar to their own, and most disappointed by limited opportunities for informal interaction with foreign scholars that might contribute to their research ($d = -.18$). They evidently had expected the organization of the congress to facilitate interaction to a greater degree than they actually found to be the case ($d = -.17$). They had expected that a wider range of viewpoints would be presented in the formal sessions and were unhappy that panel chairs did not generate more discussion ($d = -.11$). Respondents had expected that discussions, especially on contentious cold war issues, would be more free-flowing than they were ($d = -.04$).

Previous visits to the Soviet Union made a difference, albeit with apparently contradictory effects, in the degree to which what one expects is what one finds. On the one hand, in an overall sense those respondents who had been in the Soviet Union before the IPSA world congress had similar expectations to those who had not (mean scores across the 11 items = 2.68 and 2.67, respectively). What they experienced, however, was much more positive (with mean scores of 2.83 and 2.65, respectively). Previous visitors note particularly that they learned much more from Soviet and East European participants than they had anticipated ($d = +.45$) and that they found more colleagues with similar interests ($d = +.30$). First-time visitors to the Soviet Union had expected the organization of the congress to facilitate interaction more than it did ($d = -.25$) and found their opportunities for contacts with foreign scholars more limited ($d = -.21$). If, on the other hand, we turn to individual correlation coefficients for each of the eleven items, then we discover that the match between expectations and experiences is greater for previous visitors ($r = .52$) than for first-time visitors ($r = .38$). What these data suggest is that previous visits give individual assessments greater congruence, but leave the aggregate of those who made them a bit more pessimistic about the opportunities provided by the IPSA meetings than their subsequent experience warranted. The congress provided more opportunities for interaction than they had dared hope.

Looking at the home country of the participants does not add much to our understanding of the congress's impact. Overall, North Americans and participants from other Western countries report sets of expectations and experiences that are close to the average. The former indicate that they were somewhat better able to make contacts with Soviet citizens than they had expected ($d = +.17$)—possibly because of a concerted effort by some North Americans to meet with Soviet dissidents and Jews. Other Westerners found it easier than they had anticipated to meet with Soviet and East European scholars ($d = +.18$ and $+.22$, respectively). By contrast, political scientists from the Third World found things overall slightly worse than they had thought they would be. They are particularly disappointed that the congress's organization did not better facilitate interaction ($d = -.30$) and that they did not have more opportunities to meet foreign scholars ($d = -.25$). Correlations by region of aggregated mean scores across the 11 items indicate only slight differences, and virtually none between North Americans and other Westerners in terms of their expectations ($r = .98$) and experiences ($r = .97$).

Classifying respondents according to their professional and international skills and activity provides some additional clues. In no case, however, as Table 4.2 indicates, does a statistically significant degree of correlation explain much variance in individual responses. Perhaps the most interesting classification is the participants' record of previous attendance at IPSA world congresses. By and large, those who had attended several such congresses went to Moscow with fairly low expectations about what they would encounter, and are most positive about the professional contacts they actually made there and the organizational aspects of the congress itself. The more internationally competent participants are, the more likely they were to expect and experience opportunities for contacts with foreign scholars and, more generally, other participants with research interests similar to their own. Enjoying high professional status seems to be the best predictor of whether or not respondents will establish contacts with Soviet and East European scholars. Those with high professional status are also more likely to conclude that the organization of the congress facilitated informal interaction. In meeting Soviet scholars, possessing international research skills or a record of international scholarly activity seemed to help; while past experience with IPSA world congresses and high levels of professional activity were conducive to meeting East European scholars. Those with an international orientation, whether in the form of skills or activities (including attending IPSA world congresses), are least likely to have found the Moscow meetings a satisfying experience.

The data suggest *in fine* different but compatible findings according to whether we are looking at individual participants or at the aggregate of respondents to the survey. At the individual level, those who went to Moscow found pretty much what they expected to find. This is especially the case for those with prior experience in the Soviet Union, and with respect to such matters as contacts with the Soviet people, accommodations, and the Moscow meetings as a whole. But even these respondents report some surprises, most notably the fact that they learned more professionally from the Soviet and East European participants than they had anticipated. Further, levels of professional and international involvement are clearly associated with the individual respondents' expectations and experiences. Those higher on various scales tended to have lower expectations and more positive experiences than did the remainder.

At the aggregate level, expectations and experiences were both fairly high. Averaging the mean responses shown in Table 4.1 for the categories most directly relevant to scientific impact (that is, omitting contacts with the Soviet people, accommodations, and general satisfaction), we find that, overall, the experience of the congress (2.65) slightly exceeded expectations (2.63). Respondents were most dubious about their prospects for meeting East Europeans and, while the level of contacts they experienced was still not very high, it was substantially higher than what they had anticipated. They

Table 4.2 Expectations, Experiences, and Professional Activity
Correlation Coefficients ($p < .10$)

Participants who are very active internationally reported:	
Low experience of overall satisfaction	−.22***
Low expectation of overall satisfaction	−.14**
Low experience of adequate accommodations	−.11*
Low expectation of adequate accommodations	−.08*
Low expectation of prof. learning from Soviet/E.Eur. scholars	−.07*
High expectation of contacts with foreign scholars	+.07*
High experience of contacts with Soviet scholars	+.08*
Participants who are highly competent internationally reported:	
Low expectation of prof. learning from Soviet/E.Eur. scholars	−.10*
Low experience of overall satisfaction	−.08*
High expectation of participants with similar research interests	+.09*
High experience of contacts with Soviet scholars	+.09*
High experience of participants with similar research interests	+.09*
High experience of contacts with foreign scholars	+.14**
High expectation of contacts with foreign scholars	+.20***
Participants who have attended several IPSA world congresses reported:	
Low expectation of contact with Soviet people	−.16**
Low experience of contact with Soviet people	−.13**
Low expectation of prof. learning from Soviet/E.Eur. scholars	−.12**
Low expectation of overall satisfaction	−.12*
Low experience of overall satisfaction	−.12*
Low expectation of adequate accommodations	−.10*
Low experience of adequate accommodations	−.09*
High experience panel chairs encourage free discussion	+.07*
High experience of participants with similar research interests	+.08*
High experience of contacts with East European scholars	+.09*
High expectation Congress org. would facilitate interaction	+.10*
High experience of contacts with foreign scholars	+.11*
Participants who have been very active professionally reported:	
Low expectation of prof. learning from Soviet/E.Eur. scholars	−.09*
Low expectation of free discussion in sessions	−.08*
High expectation of contacts with East European scholars	+.08*
High experience of contacts with East European scholars	+.09*
Participants with substantial professional status reported:	
Low expectation of free discussion in sessions	−.08*
High expectation of participants with similar research interests	+.08*
High experience Congress org. facilitated interaction	+.08*
High expectation of contacts with East European scholars	+.11*
High experience of contacts with East European scholars	+.11*
High experience of contacts with Soviet scholars	+.13**

Significance levels: * = $p < .10$; ** = $p < .01$; *** = $p < .001$.

are disappointed that the organization of the congress did not facilitate interaction to a greater extent, and that there were inadequate opportunities for informal interaction with participants from other countries and insufficient formal interaction in the panel sessions. We shall return later in this chapter and in Chapter 6 to some organizational problems and suggestions for improvement.

Such problems notwithstanding, most respondents (91%) are either very or somewhat satisfied with the IPSA world congress as a whole. On a four-point scale (from "not at all satisfied" = 1 to "very satisfied" = 4), the mean score for the entire sample of those who went to Moscow is 3.38. North Americans are particularly pleased (3.46), while other Westerners and Third World participants are less so (3.30 and 3.28, respectively). The higher individuals score on our various scales of professionalism and internationalism, the more likely it is that they rate their experience in Moscow as very satisfactory: international activity ($r = .19, p < .001$); IPSA experience ($r = .15, p < .01$); professional activity ($r = .13, p < .01$); professional status ($r = .10, p < .10$); and international competence ($r = .09, p < .10$). All these figures correspond well to the findings reported in Table 4.1, both that respondents had high expectations regarding their visit to Moscow and that these expectations were by and large realized.

Soviet Government and People

A purpose of traveling abroad is to learn something about foreign lands and people. Political scientists attending a meeting in Moscow, we might expect, would be particularly keen to observe the Soviet political system at work. But how were they supposed to do this? Except for those with relatives or acquaintances in the Soviet Union whom they could visit, or those who had appropriate linguistic skills, possibilities for meaningful contacts were limited. Linguistic and perhaps other barriers made it difficult for political scientists from nonsocialist countries even to meet with their Soviet colleagues over breakfast or in the hotel lounge. It is no wonder that many participants lament the infrequency of contacts with Soviet citizens and scholars.

Even so, opportunities for a firsthand glimpse at life in the Soviet Union existed. At a casual level, interaction with hotel staff and tourist-shop personnel, along with observations made on the streets or in the subway, may have produced some useful insights. A number of participants made a point of visiting coreligionists or known Soviet dissidents. Some also took advantage of visits organized by the Soviet Political Science Association to government officials, daycare centers, and the like, or went on guided tours to other parts of the Soviet Union. Then, too, all were touched by the organizational aspects of the congress and probably most attended several panel sessions at Moscow State University. The impressions gained of Soviet life and society were doubtless fragmentary, but perhaps not more so than those of other countries obtained in the course of IPSA world congresses elsewhere.

Images

Most participants, we have hypothesized, went to the IPSA world congress in Moscow with a fairly concrete image of the Soviet Union, that is, some picture in their minds of what they believed to be true. Images correspond only more or less to reality. But, since we often form attitudes and take action on the basis of our images, the content of those images is an important variable in studying the political behavior of individuals and groups.

We asked our respondents to engage in an intellectual game: to try (in 1980) to recall what image they had held of the Soviet Union before attending the world congress in August 1979, and then to specify how the experience during the course of their visit affected that image. More particularly, did the experience reinforce the respondent's pre-existing image, leave it unchanged, or significantly change it? With what impressions did congress participants return to their home countries after a brief sojourn in the Soviet Union?

Exposure to life in the Soviet Union had a widely varying effect on the participants' images. Responses to the overall question of changed images fall roughly equally in all three categories: 30 percent think that being in the Soviet Union merely reinforced the images they already enjoyed, while the remainder are split evenly between those finding no change and those finding at least some change (35 percent each). On a three-point scale (ranging from reinforcement = -1 over no change = 0 to change = +1), the average score is +.05—a very slight change. Of the various categories into which we classified our respondents, the most interesting in this respect comprise participants from the Third World, whose images changed fairly substantially (average score = +.31), and those who had participated in many previous IPSA world congresses, who tend to find their earlier images reinforced (average score = -.26).

Those whose views were reinforced only infrequently report the reasons for this. Most say that they were already fairly familiar with the Soviet Union, either from previous visits or extensive reading, or else that the experience of visiting Moscow and perhaps participating in a tour enhanced the complexity of their images without changing their overall tenor. Of respondents in the latter category, most cite information critical of the Soviet

Union. Only three respondents reporting reinforced images cite positive developments. One expressed the belief that the Soviet Union is "more open to contact and discussion" than previously experienced, another reported the discovery that one's Soviet colleagues are "more sophisticated, more open-minded" than previously thought, and the third observed that "whatever their discontents, people seem to feel their leaders know how to control the economy and that life is growing gradually better."

The responses of those whose images had changed are much more variegated. Some were "impressed by the achievements of the country," or became "more aware of internal pluralism" or other developments. Others were, in the words of one of them, "surprised at how much freedom we were allowed compared to my previous visits." A majority, however, found the domestic circumstances in the Soviet Union even worse than they had imagined.

Attitudes

Subsequent questions asked whether and how attending the IPSA world congress changed the respondent's attitude toward the Soviet government and the people of the Soviet Union. About two in seven (29%) report attitudinal changes with respect to the government, and three in seven (43%) with respect to the people. The overall changes are nonetheless in opposite directions. Using a five-point scale (from an attitude change very much in a negative direction = -2 over neutral = 0 to an attitude change very much in a positive direction = +2), we find the average shifts to be negative for the government (-.28) and positive for the people (+.40). North Americans became much more positive about the Soviet people (+.49) than did participants from other Western countries and the Third World (+.29 each). Similarly, political scientists who attended many previous IPSA world congresses distinguish themselves from others who are highly professional in their orientation: Those with extensive IPSA experience are the only ones with a below-average negative shift in attitudes toward the government (-.26) and a substantially higher-than-average positive shift in attitudes toward the Soviet people (+.70).

Reasons offered by respondents to explain their change in attitude toward the Soviet government parallel those summarized above regarding changed images. Persons with more negative attitudes criticize what they saw as controls on the movement of people (including participants in the IPSA world congress), the prevalence of petty corruption, rigid adherence by Soviet scholars to the government's ideological line, excessive bureaucracy, and, more generally, a governmental system that, as one respondent says, "simply does not work." Others express more positive shifts in attitude. "I liked the emphasis placed on education, art, sports, health, housing projects (still below present needs), etc.," writes one political scientist. Another merely notes that the government enjoys "wide acceptance among people; multiracial society; sense of communism as an *indigenous* ideology widely accepted." But, for the most part, the written comments support the coded ratings reported earlier: A firsthand view of the Soviet government in action did not elicit positive views among political scientists attending the IPSA world congress.

Quite a different picture emerges with respect to the Soviet people. Some respondents criticize an apparent surliness and rigidity, but most express greater understanding for Soviet citizens' response to their lot in life. A few find the "Soviet people more freeminded and accessible" than expected; "they talk of liberalization and expect democratic communism." Other characterizations abound: obedient, warm, docile, hospitable, apathetic, decent, male-chauvinistic, generous, suspicious of foreigners, culturally rich, perversely pleased with their suffering, and withal friendly. Some who had toured the Caucausus or Soviet Asia also comment on the "national pride and distinctiveness" of the various Soviet peoples.

In short, taking into account the possibility that our respondents did not make the clear distinctions between "images" and "attitudes" that we had intended, and considering that what some saw as reinforcement of pre-existing images others interpreted as significant change, a fairly coherent picture of changes in perspectives becomes visible. Those without previous experience in the Soviet Union gained a substantial amount of information to fill out and temper their views. The nature of the situation doubtless precluded substantial change. After all, most congress participants were in the Soviet Union for only 1 or perhaps 2 weeks, and were exposed more to problems of daily life (such as unexpected controls and unresponsive bureaucracies) than to the larger picture of life and politics in the Soviet Union. Moreover, their contact with common Soviet citizens was for the most part superficial. What resulted was marginal rather than spectacular change. Congress participants as a whole became slightly more convinced of the shortcomings of the Soviet system of governance, and more sympathetic toward the common citizens (albeit not the *nomenclatura*) who must cope on a daily basis and throughout their lives with that system.

International Scientific Networking

A basic justification for scientific congresses is that they further scholarly activities by bringing together disciplinary leaders who can learn from one another. Indeed, it is the opportunity to develop and maintain contacts that respondents cite as the single most important function of national scientific congresses for individual participants (Table 3.5). It follows that international scientific congresses should facilitate cross-national learning. We would expect those attending such conferences not only to develop contacts especially with colleagues from other countries and to learn something from interactions with others, but also subsequently to keep in touch with new colleagues met at the congress. Networks of international contacts help the individual scholar keep up-to-date on new lines of research in other parts of the world. They also provide sources of valuable information, possibilities for future meetings, and perhaps even scholarly collaboration.

To what extent did the Moscow world congress facilitate this process? To answer this question we shall look first at the kinds of informal contacts that respondents report having had with various categories of other participants in the congress. Table 4.3 shows the aggregate scores for each category. It reveals that participants were most likely to meet informally with colleagues from their own country, and least likely to enjoy informal contacts with Soviet and East European scholars. The degree of respondents' international competence is modestly associated with Soviet contacts; and those with IPSA experience are the most apt to have informal contacts with East European scholars.

The regional origin of respondents shows some interesting diversity in this respect. Of the three regional groupings that received questionnaires, participants from the Third World are the most isolated in terms of both the contacts they have with others and the likelihood that North American and other Western scholars have contacts with them. A certain asymmetry in North-South communication is apparent. Whereas the aggregate Third World score for contacts with Western Europeans and North Americans stands at 3.33 (slightly under the score of contacts with scholars from their own country), the reverse scores are 2.65 for North Americans and 2.28 for Western Europeans. The relatively smaller number of registrants from the Third World (perhaps 194—but see Table 1.2—as opposed to 305 North Americans and 432 other Westerners) may account in part for this finding, for there were fewer Third World participants with whom the latter could meet. The lower part of Table 4.3 nonetheless suggests that other factors were at work as well. Highly professional and internationally active political scientists seem to gravitate more toward East Europeans and especially Westerners than toward Third World participants.

Do participants try to keep up contacts with colleagues they met for the first time in Moscow? As Table 4.4 indicates, considerable effort was expended. Correspondence with Western Europeans is most common: Half, that is, 184 of the 369 respondents who went to Moscow report such an activity. Almost as many (182, or 49 percent) corresponded with North Americans they met at the congress. In general, political scientists made the greatest effort to maintain contacts with colleagues in Western Europe (1.51

Table 4.3 Informal Contacts Established at IPSA World Congress, Moscow, 1979

	Region of Those with Whom Contacts Established				
Category of Respondent	Own Country	Soviet	Other E. Eur.	W. Eur. No. Am.	Third World
A. *Scale Scores*					
North Americans	3.64	2.44	2.45	3.29	2.65
Other Westerners	3.59	2.35	2.51	3.48	2.28
Third World	<u>3.36</u>	<u>2.31</u>	<u>1.97</u>	<u>3.33</u>	<u>2.28</u>
Total	3.59	2.39	2.43	3.37	2.52
B. *Correlation Coefficients*					
International Activity	−.13**	+.05	+.12*	+.23***	+.09*
International Competence	−.12**	+.08*	+.15**	+.19***	+.00
IPSA Experience	−.04	+.03	+.19***	+.19***	+.06
Professional Activity	+.04	−.00	+.12*	+.11*	+.01
Professional Status	−.04	+.05	+.15**	+.06	+.08*

Note: Aggregate scores based on the scale: No contact at all = 1; very little contact = 2; occasional contact = 3; great deal of contact = 4. Significance levels: * = $p < .10$; ** = $p < .01$; *** = $p < .001$.

contacts per participant), followed by those in North America (1.43), the Soviet Union and Eastern Europe (1.04), and, in last place, the Third World (0.69). Only 82 respondents (22%) report that they made no successful efforts to keep up with colleagues from Western Europe they originally met in Moscow, and only 54 (15%) failed to pursue any contacts from North America. The number of congress participants who made no effort to keep up with Eastern European contacts is about the same as that for the Third World (123 and 121, respectively, or 33 percent).

Figures for the number of contacts per participant, shown in Table 4.4, provide some indication of the extent to which the various groupings of participants maintain the contacts they made at the congress. Other Westerners are somewhat more active in this regard than are North Americans or participants from the Third World. Those who score high on the various scales of professionalism and internationalism have with but one exception (namely, the efforts of scholars with high professional status to maintain contacts with colleagues in the Third World) better than average records.

These results indicate substantial activity aimed at establishing and maintaining contacts: At least half of those attending the Moscow world congress pursued one or more contacts made there. Although most activity occurred among North Americans and other Westerners, a quarter of the political scientists report that they corresponded with at least one colleague

Table 4.4 Efforts to Keep Up with Colleagues Originally Met in Moscow

	Location			
	USSR & E. Eur.	Western Europe	Third World	North America
A. Modes of maintaining contacts, all participants				
I have not tried to keep up contacts	123	78	121	49
My attempts have been unsuccessful	23	4	9	5
Total: no contacts	146	82	130	54
Through correspondence	139	184	92	182
Scientific meetings, conferences	43	88	33	79
Visits or exchange of visits	46	61	24	58
Exchange of reprints, papers	111	151	74	145
Joint or parallel research	20	40	15	40
Joint publication	19	32	13	23
Other	6	3	2	2
Total: contacts	384	559	253	529
Contacts per participant (n = 369)	1.04	1.51	0.69	1.43
B. Contacts per participant for various participant groupings				
North American participants (n = 193)	1.07	1.34	0.70	1.34
Other Western participants (n = 140)	1.16	1.78	0.61	1.55
Third World participants (n = 36)	0.42	1.39	0.86	1.47
High international activity (n = 74)	1.27	1.91	0.88	1.74
High international competence (n = 153)	1.23	1.97	0.79	1.81
High IPSA experience (n = 23)	1.35	2.61	0.70	2.04
High professional activity (n = 88)	1.36	2.03	0.86	1.70
High professional status (n = 143)	1.32	1.59	0.67	1.48
Total (n = 369)	1.04	1.51	0.69	1.43

from the Third World whom they met for the first time in Moscow, and almost two-fifths claim they wrote to newly established contacts in the USSR and Eastern Europe. The fact that 139 (or 38 percent of the sample) managed to correspond with Soviet and East European scholars they met at the congress, that 111 exchanged papers, 46 exchanged visits, and 20 initiated joint research projects with them is notable in view of the various obstacles to such ties.

Modifications in Scholarly Behavior

How and to what extent did the experience of the IPSA world congress affect the work of those scholars who attended? A little less than a quarter (23%) of the respondents report that, considering the congress as a whole and all their interactions with congress participants, they received information that led to a major modification in their professional activities. Of these respondents, 75 percent indicate that the information came from informal contacts, 40 percent mention papers they read and almost that many papers they heard presented (35%), and a third (33%) cite floor discussion in panel sessions. Over three-quarters (77%) state that this new information modified their research, and somewhat fewer than a third see an impact on their teaching and plans for publication (32 percent each). Only a handful mentions applied work (6%) or administration (4%).

Three points stand out when we look at how various groupings of respondents consider their work modified by the experience of participating in the Moscow world congress. First, scholars from the Third World are the most likely to see modifications (38%), especially through reading papers or hearing them presented orally; each one reporting a modification refers to his or her research and almost half (46%) to teaching. Second, North Americans are more likely to report a major modification than are other Western participants (23 and 16 percent, respectively). Indeed, over half (45 of 81) of all those who experienced such an impact are from the United States and Canada. More than two-thirds of these North Americans (31 of 45) say that what they learned at the congress affects their research and half that many (16) refer to their teaching. Third, the grouping least likely to report any such modification comprises those who attended the greatest number of previous IPSA world congresses (8 percent, or 2 of the 24 participants who attended at least 4 of the 5 triennial congresses between 1964 and 1976).

Asked what the nature of these modifications is, those reporting them emphasize intellectual contributions. Thus 43 percent, or 37 of the 85 responses (up to 3 of which were recorded for each respondent), say that the congress gave them new insights, perspectives, or interests. Another fifth report either that the congress resulted in a change of emphasis, focus, or approach (11%) or that it helped them to clarify or better to understand certain issues (9%). About the same number (19%) points to new materials, techniques, or sources, while the remainder (17%) mentions such practical considerations as collaboration, publication, and travel opportunities.

A comparison of political scientists with psychologists and sociologists who in 1966 attended their own world congresses (Johns Hopkins University, 1968)—in Moscow and Evian, France, respectively—shows some interesting similarities and differences with respect to modifications in their work (Table 4.5).[1] The number of political scientists reporting major modifications in *any* area of professional activity (23 percent of all who attended) corresponds roughly to that of sociologists (21 percent of whom report changes in their subject matter area, 10 percent in some other area of activity) and psychologists (18 and 13 percent, respectively). Taking the number of

Table 4.5 Impact of World Congresses on Participants' Scientific Work: A Comparison of Psychologists, Sociologists, and Political Scientists

	Int'l. Psych. Ass'n 1966	Int'l. Sociol. Ass'n 1966	Int'l. Pol.Sci. Ass'n 1979
Activities Modified			
Research	22%	24%	17%
Teaching	5	3	7
Publication	1	<1	7
Applied work	2	2	1
Administration	–	<1	1
Theoretical work	2	–	–
Other and unspecified	2	2	–
Total	34	32	33
Sources of Modification			
Oral presentation	14	10	8
Written copy of paper	3	–	9
Session discussion	6	8	7
Informal contacts	8	11	16
Other and unspecified	6	<1	1
Total	37	30	41
Nature of Modification			
New scientific knowledge:			
New insights	4	3	10
Theory construction	2	–	–
New emphasis	6	6	2
Subtotal	(11)	(9)	(12)
Enhancement of ongoing activities			
Clarification	4	6	2
Initiate new type of related work	9	7	–
New materials, techniques	11	5	4
Intensify present work	8	12	–
Subtotal	(33)	(31)	(6)
Other			
Publication, collaboration	1	<1	2
Conference visits	–	–	2
Other and unspecified	3	1	<1
Subtotal	(4)	(1)	(5)
Total	48	41	23

Note: The IPA and ISA asked slightly different questions of authors vs. other attendants and reported the findings separately (see Johns Hopkins University, 1968: 11, 12, 21, 38, 39, 47); the IPSA questionnaire asked both authors and others the IPA/ISA's questions for attendants. The data reported here on activities modified and nature of the modification combine the two sets of responses for IPA and ISA respondents.

overlapping categories into account, these figures are all in the same range, that is, roughly a quarter. The following is a brief summary of some of the other findings.

1. Activities modified: Each of the three sets of respondents emphasizes major changes in their research as a result of attending world congresses. Political scientists are less likely than the others to stress research, and more likely to point to impacts on their teaching and publication.

2. Sources of modification: While some of the differences may be artifacts of alternative modes of scientific discourse—for example, the average length of papers, which tend to be longer in political science meetings, and hence the relative emphasis on reading papers vs. hearing them presented—the importance of informal contacts for political scientists stands out clearly.

3. Nature of modification: By grouping the responses into three categories—new scientific knowledge (new insights, new emphasis, theory construction), enhancement of ongoing activities (clarification, initiation of new type of related work, new materials or techniques, intensification of present work), and other (publication and collaboration, conference visits, and other)—we find a very sharp difference. Whereas both psychologists and sociologists are apt to stress the congress's contribution to thought and work in process (69 and 76 percent, respectively, of their responses), political scientists place greater weight on new insights and emphases (52 percent of their responses).[2]

Despite major similarities, then, political scientists see the impact of their world congress somewhat more in terms of their teaching and publication, stress the importance of informal contacts, and learned something they describe in more than incremental terms.

Improving Scientific Communication at World Congresses

To note that our respondents found the IPSA world congress valuable for scientific communication is not to say that they see no room for improvement. An indication of this came in response to our question about the best and worst panels respondents attended (see Chapter 5 for details). Almost a quarter of the responses (24%) citing a "best" panel emphasize the quality of discussion, interaction among scholars with diverse points of view, or some similar characteristic. Another 15 percent single out the benefits of exchanges between East Europeans and Western scholars in particular. Over half the reasons given in identifying the "worst" panel have political overtones. Concern with the inhibiting effect of politics and ideology on the scholarly exchange of views, however, points directly at the need for a firmer hand to keep the sessions on the proper intellectual track.

We then asked our respondents if they had encountered problems of scientific communication that could be corrected in future world congresses. Of the 369 respondents who went to Moscow, fewer than half (46%) report running into such problems, and they made some 204 suggestions for improvement. By contrast, psychologists and sociologists evaluating their own world congresses of 1966 provided many more suggestions of this sort (respectively, 2.5 and 2.7 times as many suggestions per respondent).

Table 4.6, which compares the reactions of the three sets of respondents, reveals rather different sets of concerns. (In fact, the Pearsonian correlation coefficients between IPSA participants on the one hand and IPA and ISA participants on the other are, respectively, .21 and .40; that between IPA and ISA participants is .77.) Some of these differences are fundamental. Political scientists, for instance, are happier with the general organization and format of their meeting than are psychologists and sociologists. They are far more distressed than the others, however, by the intrusion of politics into their proceedings. Other differences doubtless stem from technical issues. Thus the large number of suggestions regarding the distribution of papers at the political science and sociological meetings may indicate a particular problem rather than a general one.

Yet in another way the three sets of reactions, together with the suggestions made by these scholars, present a congruent picture. They constitute an inventory of structural, organizational, and substantive characteristics of the ideal world congress.

First, a good program must be well planned in advance. The most disgruntled in this respect are the sociologists, over half (51%) of whom make suggestions for improvement. Most emphasize the general importance of advance planning and distribution of the program, while 7 percent mention a need for more opportunities for informal discussion. Somewhat under half of the psychologists (46%) are concerned enough about organization and format to suggest alternative procedures. Almost half of these in turn (22%) want more opportunities for informal discussion or a larger number of small meetings for persons working in specific areas. This need evidently becomes more critical as the size of a meeting increases. Nine percent of the sociologists address the problem of size directly by suggesting that attendance be restricted. The remainder of the psychologists' and sociologists' responses in this general category are distributed over many practical suggestions, such as avoiding the simultaneous scheduling of sessions having related subject matter. By contrast, a much smaller proportion of political scientists (9%) singles out communication problems at the IPSA world congress. Other matters seem to concern them more.

Second, attention should be paid to the conduct of the panels, generally

Table 4.6 Suggestions for Improving Future World Congresses: Views of Psychologists, Sociologists, and Political Scientists

	International Psychological Association (1966)		International Sociological Association (1966)		International Political Science Association (1979)	
	% of Respondents (N=467)	% of Total Responses	% of Respondents (N=476)	% of Total Responses	% of Respondents (N=369)	% of Total Responses
Improve general organization and format	46%	35%	51%	34%	9%	16%
(More opportunities for informal discussion)	(22)	(16)	(7)	(5)	(4)	(7)
Improve paper distribution	8	6	32	22	14	25
Improve conduct of panels	37	28	30	20	11	20
(More panel time for discussion)	(10)	(8)	(7)	(5)	(3)	(5)
Reduce language difficulties	30	23	21	14	11	20
Reduce politics	2	1	1	1	8	15
Improve other facilities	10	8	13	9	2	4
Total	133%	100%	148%	100%	55%	100%

Note: Multiple responses permitted. Percentages may not add up because of rounding. IPA and ISA data recalculated from Johns Hopkins University (1968: 25-27, 50-52).

seen as the heart and soul of a scholarly meeting. The suggestion most frequently made urges a higher ratio of discussion to formal presentation in the panels. Other suggestions—stronger leadership, stricter time limits on presentations, and fewer papers per panel—aim at the same goal. Five percent of the psychologists and 1 percent of the sociologists, but none of the political scientists, call for quality controls to improve the papers; and a few in each group want improved presentations, especially urging that papers not be read (for a psychologist's suggestions, see Nuttin, 1974).

A third important concern is an improved procedure for distributing papers. Sociologists (32%) and political scientists (14%) stressing this point want a better supply of papers available at the congress (although a few urge that abstracts of all papers be distributed either before or at the congress so that participants might better gauge which panels would be most interesting).[3] Psychologists (8%), for whom this problem had apparently not been so serious, emphasize the need to distribute the papers before the congress.

Fourth, language barriers should be reduced. Most suggestions refer to the need for better capabilities for simultaneous translation, and, especially for political scientists, greater availability of headsets.[4] (Ten political scientists but no psychologists or sociologists argue that the language problem could be easily solved by using English only.) Six percent of the sociologists think it would be useful to extend simultaneous translation to the smaller workshops. An equal number of sociologists and 5 percent of the psychologists suggest interpreters for informal person-to-person discussion.

Finally, a world congress should stick to science, not politics. Some 8 percent of the IPSA participants express a concern with clarifying the role of the host country to avoid interference and ensure discussion. A much smaller number of psychologists (2%), who had also met in Moscow, recommend "separating ideological discourse from science" or "eliminating politicking." About half as many sociologists voice similar notions.

Individual Learning

The findings outlined above suggest that the impact of international scientific congresses on their participants' intellectual development and scholarly work is more cumulative and subtle than immediate and dramatic. Roughly a third of our respondents claim to have changed their image of the Soviet Union as a result of their experience in Moscow, but the changes reported are for the most part marginal rather than basic. All in all, the participants' attitudes became more negative vis-à-vis the Soviet government and more sympathetic toward the Soviet people.

Images, Attitudes, and International Understanding

A vast array of social-psychological studies on the effects of foreign travel, overseas study, and the like urges caution in interpreting such findings (see Kelman, 1965). For one thing, we should note that some 65 percent report no change in their images and roughly the same proportions record no changes in their attitudes toward the Soviet government (71%) or people (57%). This fact suggests relatively little movement in terms of images and attitudes. Still, a third or so—some 350 political scientists if we extrapolate our findings to all participants from nonsocialist countries—is a sizable number. This is especially so if we consider that, memory being what it is, many respondents filling out the questionnaire in fall 1980 may well have forgotten what they learned in summer 1979.

We must be particularly wary about overinterpreting the finding of improved attitudes toward the Soviet people. It need not mean that the respondents "like" these people more. Taken in conjunction with a more negative view of the government, it may only indicate that they have a greater understanding of the circumstances in which Soviet citizens live and hence look on them with greater admiration. International exchanges of various sorts ultimately aim more at understanding than affection. We have no reason to assume that a world political science congress would be any different.

By the same token, although visiting the Soviet Union in the course of attending the world congress undoubtedly broadened the intellectual map of some political scientists, it is not certain that this process had anything to do with the world congress as such. Visiting the Soviet Union in some other context might have had just as great an effect—or perhaps greater, if we take into account the amount of time that congress participants spent in scholarly sessions or with colleagues from their own country. In this sense, holding the world congress in Moscow was more an occasion for learning than its cause.

The argument that interaction among scientists at international congresses promotes international understanding and contributes toward a basis for peace is thus problematic, at least at the interpersonal level. Firsthand experience with the Soviet governmental apparatus did not lead many political scientists to view that government in a more positive light. What effect an enhanced understanding of the Soviet people's situation will have in the long run is a question our data cannot answer. Since in the future most congress participants will probably have little contact with the Soviet population, we might speculate that enhanced understanding alone will not yield much by way of concrete consequences for their attitudes toward the Soviet Union. But, then, a functional integrationist would expect ISCs to promote peace without necessarily changing attitudes toward governments. This fact raises the far more complicated question of the effect of interpersonal interaction at the scientific level.

Scientific Networks and International Understanding

The IPSA world congress provided different configurations of benefits for different groupings of participants. Third World scholars report a substantially greater-than-average degree of modification in their work activities as a result of attending the congress. But they appear to have gained least from the informal interaction of participants in Moscow. They are even more disappointed than other participants that the organization of the congress did not better facilitate this interaction. Their difficulties in becoming involved in networks of informal communication are further illustrated by the fact that other participants report fewer efforts to keep up with colleagues from the Third World than with those from Eastern Europe, Western Europe, and North America.

For veterans of previous IPSA world congresses, the reverse seems to have occurred. They report abundant opportunities for informal interaction and were the most successful grouping in establishing and maintaining new contacts. The Moscow world congress nevertheless seems to have had the least impact on the scholarly activity of these political scientists.

Generally, participants higher up the scales of professionalism and internationalism enjoy more informal interaction with colleagues from other countries than do those lower on these scales. Respondents with higher professional status are the only grouping that thinks the organization of the congress facilitated this interaction, and they report the most contact with Soviet and East European colleagues. Participants with good language skills and extensive overseas experience also report positive experiences with respect to interaction with foreign scholars during and after the congress.

Such findings suggest three points about the importance of world congresses for international scientific networking. First, by bringing new people into them and sensitizing others to their role, congresses serve to revitalize networks that have been established through overseas work and travel. Second, as the suggestions for improving world congresses amply indicate, it makes sense to modify their organization to enhance possibilities for discussion within panels and informal interaction without. Third, emerging within international political science are specialists in networking. These individuals, frequent participants in world congresses, seem to have acquired the knack for developing and maintaining contacts (although, possibly, at some cost to advances in their own research).

New Knowledge

Most participants feel that they benefitted at least to some degree from attending IPSA's world congress in Moscow. The overwhelming majority reports being at least somewhat satisfied with the experience of the congress, and almost half claim they are "very satisfied." This does not mean, of course, that they are bereft of suggestions for improving such meetings. In fact they named quite a few. Most suggestions underscore the participants' commitment to IPSA world congresses as a significant occasion for scientific communication, and many are cued directly to the development of international scientific networks.

For one of every four participants in the Moscow world congress, however, the occasion was more than a networking affair. They point to some specific way in which attending the congress significantly affected an aspect of their scholarly work. (The validity of the finding is strengthened by the fact that a similar figure obtains in other disciplines as well; in fact, we might reasonably assume that in each case the actual percentage is considerably higher, since people frequently forget the precise source of a new idea or research orientation.) About a sixth (17%) refer specifically to research as the aspect of work most significantly affected.

Although this may at first examination seem to be a modest result, it is of some consequence. Even one truly new idea or orientation can transform the face of a scientific discipline. The fact that informal contacts pursued during the congress were more important in changing these scholars' work than were the papers presented in the panels or even the formal discussions is instructive for the organization of future world congresses.

Notes

1. Some differences between the study conducted by the Center for Research in Scientific Communication of Johns Hopkins University (1968) and ours should be noted. First, of course, the IPSA world congress took place 13 years after the other two. From 1966 to 1979 the context of international science changed substantially, as East and West moved toward détente.

Second, they differed in size and composition. The 18th International Congress of Psychology, held in Moscow, was attended by 4,215 participants from 44 countries. Of these participants, more than a third (36%) came from the Soviet Union and a fifth (20%) from the United States. The 6th World Congress of Sociology, held in Evian, France, was with approximately 2,000 participants closer in size to the IPSA world congress. It was much less dominated than the psychology meetings by scholars from the Soviet Union (4%) and the United States (8%). In contrast, 18 percent of the IPSA world congress participants were from the USSR and 16 percent from the United States.

Third, the large number of psychologists meant using a sampling procedure, whereas the surveys of sociologists and political scientists used a universal sample (albeit, for the latter, only those from nonsocialist states); the surveys of psychologists and sociologists sent separate questionnaires to papergivers and other participants.

Finally, since the purposes of the studies differed, they pursued different lines of inquiry. In some cases, however, the questions were identical: on the impact of the congress on work activity, scientific communication problems encountered, and suggestions for preventing such problems in the future.

2. The unavailability of raw data from the IPA and ISA world congresses makes it difficult to specify this finding in greater detail. If, however, we view the individual response categories in Table 4.5 as percentages of the total set of modifications listed (which, of course, are also percentages), then the point made in the text appears even more clearly. For the psychologists 61 percent and, for the sociologists, 79 percent of the responses point to enhancement, whereas only 27 percent of those made by political scientists do so. By the

same token, whereas 55 percent of the political scientists' responses refer to new scientific knowledge, only 23 and 21 percent, respectively, of the responses made by psychologists and sociologists are in this category. This finding may say more about the relative degrees of acceptance of research paradigms in the three professions than anything else.

3. In fact, a book of abstracts was prepared for the IPSA meetings in Moscow (Merritt and Smirnov, 1979-1981); technical problems, however, prevented the Soviet organizing committee from producing copies for general circulation in time for the congress itself, so they were published afterwards. Such books of abstracts were distributed at the outset of the congresses in Rio de Janeiro (1982) and Paris (1985).

4. English and French are the working languages of IPSA sessions. Normally, simultaneous translation is provided only for plenary sessions. In Moscow, however, all sessions set up by the IPSA program committee (as opposed to those organized by IPSA research committees, IPSA study groups, or individual members) permitted Russian and hence required simultaneous translation. Competition for scarce headsets nevertheless became a source of irritation; on this and related points, see the exchange between Urban (1980) and Merritt (1980).

FIVE
Politics at Play

International scientific congresses, we postulated in Chapter 1, serve a multiplicity of functions for national societies. Not all these functions may be equally manifest. Moreover, the societies' governments may have widely varying perspectives on the importance of the functions they perceive. One may actively court ISCs in the hope of attracting prestige or tourist receipts, while another is blithely unaware that an international congress is taking place on its soil. One government may seek to prevent ISCs from going to certain countries, or bar its scientists from attending such meetings, while another pays scant attention to where its scientists are doing what.

From time to time the political function ISCs ostensibly serve becomes paramount in the thinking of government officials and scientists alike. This is not to say that other functions drop out of sight, and in Chapter 3 we dealt with our respondents' views on some of these other functions. The point is rather that, in certain circumstances, the political context of a world congress outweighs all others. The following are possible scenarios.

1. As during the hottest days of the cold war, implacable hostility between two blocs of states makes joint conferences impracticable and forces nonaligned states to make choices between competing congresses
2. An interest group—ethnic, political, terrorist, or whatever—below the level of the government finds the congress an opportunity to pursue its own goals
3. An issue of international political import seizes the imagination of participants, who turn the congress into an occasion to inveigh for or against the policies of given states
4. Specific quarrels, such as an association's decision to locate its congress in a particular country, restrictions set by the host country

on the association's freedom of action, refusal to grant entry visas to certain participants, or manipulation of the congress itself for the government's own purposes, arise to generate divisive strife.

Some of these actions stem from governments' intentional behavior, while others may not be under their control. Any of them, however, and still other occurrences, can cloud the scientific intent of a world congress, pushing it into the realm of international politics.

We saw in Chapter 2 that the Moscow world congress of the International Political Science Association became a political issue. In any circumstances, holding an international political science congress in Moscow is a political act. In the particular case, hostility to the Soviet Union in principle, the calls for a boycott because of the Soviet treatment of dissident scholars, struggles to secure visas for all bona fide political scientists, the view that the Soviet Union used the congress to score propagandistic points, and procedural aspects of the congress itself concatenated to focus attention on the potential or actual political functions of such congresses.

This chapter explores some central dimensions of that putative political functionality. It looks first at the extent to which political considerations played a role in our respondents' decisions to attend or not to attend the Moscow meetings. It then asks how they viewed IPSA's original decision to hold its world congress in Moscow and, more generally, whether it is ever a good idea to schedule scientific meetings in the Soviet Union. The issue of selecting sites is broadened by raising similar questions about IPSA's choices for its world congresses of 1982 and 1985. Finally, it examines participants' views about the intrusion of international politics in the actual proceedings of the congress.

To Go to Moscow or Stay Home?

As it turned out, a record number of political scientists, 1,466 in all, attended the Moscow meetings, and two-thirds of these were from nonsocialist countries. Doubtless each participant had his or her unique reason for making the journey. So did those who stayed home. With Chapter 3 having dealt with the full set of reasons for attendance or nonattendance, the question of concern here is the extent to which political scientists saw their decision to go or not to go to Moscow as an essentially political act. Among those for whom political considerations were important, was the decision an act of conscience, that is, a personal matter, or did they think that their behavior would have an impact on national governments engaged in the global arena?

Unheeded Call to Boycott

More specifically, did political scientists in nonsocialist countries, especially in the United States, boycott the IPSA world congress in Moscow for political reasons? If so, then we might expect that those who did not attend the meetings would cite political factors as the basis for their decision. To ascertain this we asked all respondents, registrants and nonregistrants alike, first whether or not they attended the Moscow world congress and, second, why they had made the choice they did.

Political reasons do not loom large in the responses of those who stayed away from the Moscow meetings. In fact, of the 62 reasons cited by those who registered for but did not attend the world congress (with multiple responses recorded separately), only 6 (10%) refer to domestic political conditions in the Soviet Union (2), its undemocratic government (2), the economic benefits that the congress would give that government (1), and the red tape entailed in getting to Moscow (1). None mentions Soviet foreign policy. The remaining respondents point to personal as well as scientific and disciplinary considerations. Asked what the *primary* reason for their decision was, an even larger fraction (91%) cites personal or scientific reasons, while only 9 percent mention political considerations.

The distribution of responses is similar for North Americans who did not register to attend the Moscow world congress. In this case, more than 11 in 12 (92%) give personal or scientific reasons for their decision (including the response that they had not heard about the world congress or were simply not interested in attending it), while only 8 percent refer to domestic or international political grounds. Half of these (4%) cite what they see as the repressive or nondemocratic character of the Soviet regime and its violation of human rights. Two percent give the Soviet government's foreign policy as the reason for not attending the congress, and another 1 percent say that they did not want to contribute to a Soviet propaganda effort.

Differences among the various subgroups in the samples exist but are insufficiently interesting from a statistical point of view to warrant much attention.[1] To put it in more technical terms: Applying the X^2-test, we were unable to reject the null hypothesis of "no difference" between nonregistrants and nonparticipant registrants in North America ($X^2 = 3.27, p > .10$), between nonparticipant North American and other registrants ($X^2 = 3.00, p > .20$), or between nonparticipant registrants from the United States and elsewhere ($X^2 = .13, p > .90$). What these relationships mean in practical terms, based on the tau-beta measure of association developed by Goodman and Kruskal, is that, even in the strongest case, between North American and other registrants, knowing the respondents' home base improves by only 3.2 percent our ability to predict what reasons they would give for not attending the Moscow meetings ($T_b = .032$). Knowing if a nonparticipant North American is a registrant or nonregistrant improves his or her predictability by 0.6 percent; and knowing whether a registrant comes from the United States or elsewhere does so by less than 0.1 percent.

In short, it was not political but primarily personal and other considerations that kept political scientists away from Moscow in 1979. This is not to ignore the fact that some saw their decisions politically motivated, still less to question the intensity of the feeling of those who shunned the Moscow meetings. The data merely show that the number of those expressing political motivations was relatively small, and suggest that their arguments did not impress many of their colleagues. Whatever the heat and smoke surrounding the matter, we can hardly speak of a serious boycott of the Moscow world congress.

Anticipated Impact of Attendance

Well, then, did political scientists think that by going to Moscow in 1979 for the IPSA world congress they would have some kind of political impact? If we look at the reasons they gave for going, then the answer to this question is a resounding "No." The proportion of participant registrants stating that their presence would make a political difference is even smaller than that of nonparticipant registrants who averred that their absence would do so. Only 2 percent of the responses given by those who went to Moscow cite either the congress's putative effect on the domestic political situation in the Soviet Union or else its more general international political consequences; about 1 in 40 participant registrants (2.6%) giving a primary reason for attending the meetings cites such considerations.[2]

Potential for Disruption

We can learn a bit more about the political scientists who expressed diverse reasons for attending or not attending the Moscow meetings by looking at their position on the five scales of professionalism and internationalism discussed in chapter 3 (see also Appendix C). As a matter of convenience, and since the data presented earlier reveal no substantial differences between them, we shall consider as a single set of responses those made by both participant and nonparticipant registrants. Table 5.1 shows separate breakdowns for *all* reasons given by those filling out our questionnaires (with as many as four responses coded per questionnaire) and the *primary* reason identified by each respondent. To facilitate comparison we shall use for each scale standardized

Table 5.1 Reasons Given for Attending or Not Attending the IPSA Moscow Meetings
Standardized Mean Scores for Scales

Scale	All Reasons Given		Primary Reason Given	
	Political	Nonpolitical	Political	Nonpolitical
Professional Status	6.1	5.9	6.9	6.0
International Competence	6.6	5.9	6.9	5.9
Professional Activity	5.1	5.9	5.7	5.9
International Activity	5.0	5.3	5.1	5.3
IPSA Experience	2.4	1.8	2.9	1.9
Average	(5.0)	(5.0)	(5.5)	(5.0)
Number of responses	19	743	13	362

Note: The actual distribution of scores on each scale was transformed into a standardized, 10-point scale by dividing the mean score of the scale by the number of points in it, and multiplying the quotient by 10.

scores ranging from 0 to 10 (Table 3.1). Table 5.1 indicates that, by way of example, for the category "all reasons given," the mean level of professional status held by those giving a political response (6.1) is slightly higher than the status of those responding in nonpolitical terms (5.9).

Several points of interest appear in Table 5.1. The most important is that respondents emphasizing political factors in their decisions on whether or not to attend the Moscow world congress generally enjoy higher levels of professional status, international competence, and IPSA experience than do those stressing personal, scientific, or disciplinary reasons. By contrast, those who underscore their scientific or disciplinary interests are more active both professionally and internationally.

These data point to a dilemma faced by those who would organize congresses for IPSA or other international scientific associations. On the one hand, the more active members tend to focus their attention on personal, scientific, or disciplinary aspects of international meetings and play down any political implications. But, on the other hand, the politically oriented scholars, though few in number, are because of their status and experience likely to be taken seriously even if their advice is not always followed. So long as an association holds its world congresses in noncontroversial countries this tension is not likely to be problematic. The dispute that broke out in summer 1978 among some members of the American Political Science Association nonetheless reveals that the tension, once unleashed, can be virulent and even disruptive.

Putting together the entire set of responses, presented both here and in Chapter 3, to the question of why political scientists did or did not visit Moscow in 1979 for the IPSA world congress points to a consistent pattern. Those who thought about it were attracted to the idea for essentially professional reasons (although tourism also played a role). What kept some of them from going were such personal factors as a lack of time, unavailability of funding, or conflicting commitments. The desire to make a political point either one way or another about the Soviet Union was important for only a very small minority. Even so, the professional standing and experience of this minority contain a potential for disruption to which IPSA organizers must be alert.

Decisionmaking About Sites

The previous section discussed the views of our respondents on an actual situation: whether or not they went to IPSA's world congress in Moscow and the reasons for their decision. Suppose, however, that we phrase the question in a somewhat more abstract vein. Given the international situation in the mid-1970s, was the decision of the International Political Science Association to hold its triennial world congress of 1979 in Moscow a good one? More generally, is it a good idea ever to hold scientific meetings in the Soviet Union?

Special Nature of Moscow as a Site

Looking retrospectively at the decision of the IPSA executive committee to hold a world congress in Moscow, by far the majority of the political scientists we questioned (80%) thinks it a good one. Again very little difference exists among the various subsets of the samples. The use of X^2-tests reveals statistically insignificant distinctions in the views expressed by those registrants who went to Moscow as opposed to those who did not, by North American registrants as opposed to nonregistrants, by North American as opposed to other registrants. Other tests indicate that knowing which category the respondents are in does not improve by much a more random procedure for predicting how they would respond to the question (T_b = .006, .005, and .007, respectively).

Political reasons play a somewhat stronger role in views on IPSA's decision than they did in the respondents' personal decision to attend or not to attend the Moscow meetings. Certainly, scientific and disciplinary reasons prevail in both cases. But about 4 in 10 respondents, irrespective of whether they think IPSA's decision good or bad, give political explanations for their views. (Proponents and opponents distribute their reasons among four general categories—scientific, personal and other, disciplinary, and political—about equally: $X^2 = 1.10, p > .70; T_b = .0005$.)

Those citing political considerations are almost four times more likely to anticipate positive political consequences than negative ones (Table 5.2). Among the 371 reasons given by respondents who think the decision to go to Moscow correct, 142 (38%) refer to domestic and international politics. Of particular importance are the prospects for international understanding that the congress might provide (49 responses, or 13 percent of all positive reasons given), expected positive social effects such as contributing to opening up or liberalizing Soviet society (8%), improved East-West communication (6%), and the need for the rest of the world to avoid isolating itself from the Soviet Union (4%). Respondents thinking the decision to go to Moscow incorrect are almost equally likely to give political reasons (38 of 106 negative responses, or 36%). The idea that an IPSA world congress could in some way help to legitimize a repressive regime weighs heaviest in their minds (17%). Almost as many cite the possibility that the Soviet Union would use the congress for propagandistic purposes (15%).

General Idea of Scientific Meetings in the Soviet Union

Roughly the same picture emerges from our examination of responses to a second, more hypothetical question: In general, is it a good idea ever to hold scientific meetings in the Soviet Union? In this case 78 percent of the 328 registrants giving definite responses (another 82 persons gave contingent responses) answered in the affirmative. Differences among participant and nonparticipant registrants from various regions and nonregistrants exist but are slight, and point in no particular direction. And roughly the same kinds of reasons for holding or not holding such meetings are offered as are used for explaining views about the correctness of IPSA's decision to go to Moscow in the first place.

A glance at Table 5.3, however, reveals another dimension of attitudes toward holding scientific meetings in the Soviet Union. Respondents who think the IPSA decision of 1976 wrong score higher on each of our five scales than do those who consider it correct; and those generally opposed to holding scientific meetings in the Soviet Union score higher on four of the five scales. The discrepancies are not great. They nonetheless underscore the point made earlier about the likelihood that political scientists will take seriously the views of opponents of such meetings if for no other reason than the fact that the latter are both active and experienced, and they enjoy high status among their professional colleagues.

Table 5.2 Political Grounds for Evaluating IPSA's Decision on Moscow

	Decision was Correct		Decision was Incorrect	
	N	%[a]	N	%[a]
Reasons referring to situation in the Soviet Union				
Broad social effects: opening up or liberalizing Soviet society	28	8		
Rejection of proposition that IPSA world congress "endorses" régime	4	1		
Positive effects vis-à-vis dissidents	2	1		
Probable Soviet use of congress for propaganda or other political purposes			16	15
Repressive, totalitarian character of Soviet régime			10	9
Congress legitimizes régime			8	8
Red tape; régime discourages participation			3	3
Total	34	9	37	35
Reasons referring to international political relations				
Foster détente, international understanding, reduction of tensions	49	13		
Importance of East-West or international communication (among countries)	23	6		
Rejection of isolation or boycott strategy as ineffective or damaging	15	4		
Acceptable under prevailing conditions	12	3		
Recognition of importance of the Soviet Union in the international system	6	2		
Congress benefits West more than East	2	1		
Positive effect on Soviet foreign policy	1	-		
Aggressive nature of Soviet foreign policy			1	1
Total	108	29	1	1
Total political references	142	38	38	36

[a]Based on total number of consistent responses (371 positive, 106 negative).

Note: For the broad categories of Soviet domestic situation vs. international political relations, $\chi^2 = 67.66$, $p < .001$; $T_b = .376$.

Table 5.3 Characteristics of Proponents and Opponents of Meetings in the USSR
Standardized Mean Scores for Scales

Scale	IPSA Decision in 1976 Correct		Generally Favor Meetings in USSR	
	Yes	No	Yes	No
Professional status	6.0	6.1	6.0	6.4
International competence	6.0	6.1	6.0	5.8
Professional activity	5.8	6.0	5.7	6.5
International activity	5.3	5.5	5.3	5.4
IPSA experience	1.0	1.3	1.6	2.6
Average	(4.8)	(5.0)	(4.9)	(5.3)
Number of responses	328	84	255	73

Note: The actual distribution of scores on each scale was transformed into a standardized, 10-point scale by dividing the mean score of the scale by the number of points in it, and multiplying the quotient by 10.

Future World Congress Sites

Bearing in mind the fact that 80 percent of our sample of registrants think that the IPSA decision to go to Moscow in 1979 was a good one, we might ask how this level of approval compares with views on other sites. At the time of the survey, the next triennial world congress, held in Rio de Janeiro in August 1982, was almost 2 years off; and members of IPSA's executive committee were already moving toward placing the world congress of 1985 in Paris. How did our respondents react to Rio de Janeiro and Paris as future sites?

Political considerations play only a small role in perspectives on the Rio meetings in 1982. More than seven in eight (88%) of those who expressed their views indicate that they were thinking of going to Rio. Only 5 percent of them refer to political conditions (of which the most frequently mentioned deal with human rights issues in Brazil). None of the 47 respondents who think that they would not attend the Rio meetings mentions political conditions. About five in six of those thinking they might attend and of those doubting they would attend the meeting in Rio indicate that their decision will rest on personal considerations, especially the availability of funding.

A question about the appropriateness of Rio de Janeiro as the site for the

IPSA world congress in 1982 elicited similar responses in some respects. Again, seven in eight (88%) of those answering express positive views. About a tenth of those respondents give politically relevant reasons, the most important of which is the view that holding the congress in Rio would recognize the role of Brazil (or Latin America) in the international political system. A handful (1%) think such a step might help open the country to liberalizing influences. Substantially more responses stress scientific (17%) or disciplinary (37%) advantages of Rio as a site. Many of these (30%) underscore the hope that holding the meeting in Rio would help to internationalize political science through exposure to more Latin American scholarship. A few simply reject the idea of political criteria for selecting sites, insisting that only scientific considerations are important or that, even if political problems abounded in Brazil, "nobody is perfect." (In the words of one respondent, "Maybe the penguins in Antarctica do not violate human rights but. . . .")

Among those who think Rio de Janeiro an inappropriate site for an IPSA world congress—46 (or 12 percent) of the 376 respondents who addressed this question—14 (31 percent of the negative responses) find political conditions in Brazil objectionable; and another 10 (22%) express doubts about whether the quality of discourse expectable at such a meeting would warrant the time and expense involved in going there. Some respondents feel that holding the congress should be made contingent on political conditions not becoming worse or on guarantees of free access to and free discussion at the meetings. The largest percentage (36%) of negative responses, however, points to the inconvenience and cost of flying to Rio de Janeiro.

Paris as a potential site for the IPSA world congress in 1985 attracts almost the same level of support (87%). A few (5%) of those favoring the site refer to such political factors as France's democratic government and its importance in international politics. Many more (46%) cite rather such positive characteristics as Paris's charm, central location, cultural amenities, and cosmopolitanism. Variations on the "I love Paris" theme are bolstered by the argument that such an attractive and acceptable site would surely encourage maximum participation. Another sixth (17%) points to the capabilities of the French to host an international conference. Only one respondent of an opposing view mentions any political factors that IPSA organizers should take into consideration before settling on Paris as the site for the world congress in 1985—that the hosts would use the congress to enhance their own prestige. Most of those opposed simply prefer some other site to Paris.

A comparison of grouped responses to questions about sites—whether or not IPSA's decision to go to Moscow was correct, and the appropriateness of Rio de Janeiro and Paris as sites for IPSA world congresses—illustrates some of the points suggested above (Table 5.4). First, the degree to which

Table 5.4 Alternative Sites for IPSA World Congresses: Views of Registrants at the Moscow Meetings

	Moscow		Rio de Janeiro		Paris	
	No	%	No	%	No	%
Appropriate	328	80	330	88	355	87
For political reasons	(143)	(38)	(39)	(10)	(19)	(5)
For other reasons	(229)	(62)	(338)	(90)	(348)	(95)
Inappropriate	84	20	46	12	53	13
For political reasons	(42)	(37)	(19)	(32)	(1)	(2)
For other reasons	(72)	(63)	(40)	(68)	(51)	(98)
Other/No response	8	–	44	–	12	–
Total	420	100	420	100	420	100

Note: The calculation of percentages omits "other," "don't know," and inconsistent responses; multiple responses were recorded.

respondents think in political terms about the three sites stands out. In no case do political considerations dominate their thinking. Second, where such considerations play a role, it varies by site. Moscow raised the hackles of a substantial minority of our respondents. This is true even among those who approve of IPSA's decision in 1976 to go to Moscow. Rio is not unproblematic, but opponents are more apt to use political arguments to justify their position than are proponents to justifying theirs. Paris is almost uncontroversial from this point of view. (Respondents who did not register to attend the Moscow meetings express views about Rio de Janeiro and Paris that are similar to those of registrants.) Third, the fact that a substantial number of registrants who disapprove of the Moscow site attended the congress anyway, together with the fact noted earlier that those registrants who did not attend withdrew for essentially nonpolitical reasons, indicates that political scientists generally place their political reservations about sites behind other considerations when deciding whether or not to attend an IPSA world congress.

More generally, the data support the idea that sites for IPSA's triennial world congresses should be rotated on a worldwide basis. This is not only a political matter deriving from the national associations' desire for equal treatment. Congresses held at different sites serve different purposes. One located in a nontraditional site may help to develop political science in that region, and give political scientists from the rest of the world an opportunity both to learn about a very different political system and to check their research findings against a different real-world context. The preference indicated by respondents for the site of the next IPSA world congress after the Paris meetings of 1985 was Tokyo, followed by New Delhi and then Beijing. Over half of the North American registrants and 38 percent of those from other Western countries mentioned locations in the Third World. The comments as a whole suggest that a system of rotation providing for geographical, cultural, and political diversity has a sound intellectual basis as well as a more political one.

Politics on the Floor

Before they went to Moscow in 1979, many political scientists from the nonsocialist world questioned the extent to which ideological or East-West disputes would creep into the congress itself. Doubtless few feared the likelihood of sharp exchanges on an intellectual plane—the confrontation of Marxism-Leninism with other philosophies of politics. The problems they foresaw lay more in stylistic elements that might stifle free discussion or the possibility that the Soviet government would manipulate the congress for its own purposes. To what extent did participants feel that these problems materialized?

There is little doubt in our respondents' minds that the Soviet government sought to use the IPSA world congress for propagandistic purposes. Three in ten (30%) agree strongly and another 5 in 10 (49%) agree somewhat with such a complaint. Only a fifth disagree somewhat (13%) or strongly (8%). Placing the responses on a four-point scale (disagree strongly = 1 to agree strongly = 4) yields an average score of 3.01, that is, very close to the response category of "some agreement." North American participants, with an average score of 3.10, are sharper in this judgment than others, but political scientists from other Western countries (2.97) and the Third World (2.83) are not far behind. Position on our various scales of professionalism and internationalism has a negligible impact on perceptions of Soviet propagandizing: The only statistically significant finding indicates that the more professionally active tend less to see any propaganda ($r = -.08, p < .10$).

There is nonetheless considerable divergency in interpreting this perception. Asked why they say the Soviet government sought to use the IPSA meetings for propagandistic purposes, over two-fifths (42%) of the 254 respondents who answered simply cite examples or define what they mean by the term. An equal percentage (42%) respond, in effect, "So what?" It was to be expected, they note, or others do it as well, or the Soviet propaganda was useless and even counterproductive. Fifteen percent evaluate the propaganda negatively. Only a third of these—5 percent of the entire sample—argues that it hindered effective communication at the congress.

But what about the intrusion of politics into individual sessions at the congress? To ascertain views on this and related matters, we asked respondents both to identify what they consider to have been the best panel and the worst panel they attended and to explain their judgment. Some 195 respondents cited a "best" panel and gave us 246 reasons for thinking so, while 123 respondents offered 152 reasons for considering a particular panel the worst. As Table 5.5 indicates (and this finding corroborates the argument of the previous chapter), the main reasons for singling out sessions for praise focus on the interest of the topic and the quality of the papers, with the organization and conduct of the session following behind. In third place are responses pointing to East-West interaction (15%) and, more rarely, the fact that politics did not intrude (3%). By contrast, in identifying why a particular panel was the worst, respondents are less apt to list scholarly matters such as interest and quality of papers or organizational issues than reasons that carry a political overtone. These last include feelings that the sessions were inhibited generally by ideological considerations (21%) or more specifically by either the behavior of Soviet participants (13%) or Soviet propaganda (12%). All in all, only about one in four of those citing reasons for a "worst" panel—a group constituting about 8 percent of all respondents who attended the Moscow meetings—found Soviet individual or governmental actions a barrier to scholarly communication.[3]

Another question approached the same issue from a slightly different direction. We asked respondents if they had encountered scientific communication problems that they believe should be corrected before the next IPSA world congress. Of the 369 respondents, less than half (46%) answered affirmatively. We have touched on some of these findings earlier. The relevant point here is that, asked to specify what had hindered effective scientific communication in Moscow, only one in eight (13%) of those making specific complaints mentions such "political" issues as interference by the host country, restrictions on free discussion in the panel sessions, or the desirability of changing the site. The number giving political responses amounts to less than six percent of all respondents who went to Moscow in 1979.

As far as their overall evaluation of the IPSA world congress is concerned, we saw that most respondents are reasonably satisfied. Placing the responses on a four-point scale (disagree strongly = 1 to agree strongly = 4) yields an average score of 3.38, that is, almost midway between "somewhat satisfied" and "very satisfied." Significantly, however, the more likely respondents are to note the propagandistic uses made of the congress by the Soviet Union, the more disgruntled they are about the congress as a whole ($r = +.28, p < .001$). Those who strongly agree with the charge of propaganda

Table 5.5 Reasons Cited for Terming a Panel Session the Best or Worst

	Best Session		Worst Session	
	N	%	N	%
Subject matter, paper quality	119	61	34	28
Organization/conduct of session	74	38	36	29
East-West considerations	37	19	61	50
East-West interaction	(29)	(15)		
Unpolitical	(5)	(3)		
Controversial	(3)	(2)		
Inhibited ideologically			(26)	(21)
Soviet speaking monopoly			(16)	(13)
Soviet propaganda			(15)	(12)
Too political			(4)	(3)
Other	16	8	21	17
Total	246	126[a]	152	124[a]
Number of respondents	195		123	

[a]Multiple responses permitted.

(N = 102) have an average evaluative score of 2.09. The remainder have quite positive scores: Respondents agreeing somewhat (N = 165), disagreeing somewhat (N = 46), or strongly disagreeing (N = 28) have scores of 3.44, 3.61, and 3.68, respectively.

Although some participants found political problems besetting the IPSA world congress in Moscow in 1979, they generally do not see them as overwhelming. Doubtless few are oblivious to the pervasive undertone of East-West politics that characterized the meetings. Most, however, find it at worst a nuisance rather than a barrier to scientific communication; and some report finding it exhilarating, a reason in itself for political scientists to meet in the Soviet Union. Only a few concentrate their criticism on Soviet scholars or their government for violating the canons of normal scientific discourse.

Impact of Politics

The data surveyed in this chapter thus suggest that the political impact of world congresses is marginal at best. This is not to say that political issues are nonexistent. First, the process of selecting a site for an IPSA world congress is at best a complicated one, and occasionally one fraught with conflict and tension. It entails negotiations ranging from persuading a national association to host the meeting all the way to laying down and enforcing the ground rules for its conduct. As the operations of the association expand in coming years, we can anticipate that the negotiating process will become ever more complex. Even so, provided that the association sticks to its basic principles—principles developed during almost four decades of activity no less than those outlined in the late 1970s—nothing inheres in this process to make it necessarily disruptive.

Second, although most members of the association prefer to see decisions about sites for world congresses as an emotionally neutral issue, one restricted to questions of how best to facilitate the international flow of scientific information, subgroups within a discipline can always challenge the political morality of a particular choice. The same is potentially true about decisions on invitations and visas, designation of speakers for plenary sessions, and a host of other matters. This disruptive potential grows as the political morality at issue captures the attention of an ever broader palette of scholars, especially if they include persons recognized as disciplinary leaders. Barring a truly momentous incident, however, few political scientists seem willing to forego the advantages derived from world congresses for the sake of political issues, even as important as those that arose in 1978-1979.

Third, governments of host countries may use congresses to toot their own horns or to achieve other domestic (or international) political purposes. But how important is this? Participants in the Moscow world congress were aware of the propagandistic purposes to which the Soviet government sought to put the meetings, and many found this behavior irritating. Relatively few, though, saw it hindering scientific communication. Many more considered it useless or counterproductive. If the primary Soviet goal was propagandizing political scientists from nonsocialist countries, then their relative imperviousness must have made the IPSA world congress in Moscow a failure from the Soviet viewpoint. Moreover, given the welter of other events competing for world attention, we must question whether the costs of politicizing a world congress are worth any political benefits in terms of a host country's foreign policy.

We would of course be hardpressed to claim that the Soviet government's efforts were fruitless in the broader framework within which it works. Televising a Soviet-organized session on Lenin, which happened to take place on the congress's last afternoon, and claiming that the session was the culmination of the congress's endeavors may well have shored up the government's overall information program for its own citizens and perhaps others. Soviet press reports emphasizing the open exchanges that took place may symbolically have supported the Soviet Union's stress on its contribution to détente. It nevertheless seems that, for the international political science community, such measures fell on deaf ears.

It would also be incorrect to suggest that, inevitably, political scientists' distaste for politicized world congresses will lead them to ignore genuinely contentious issues. In fact, in the midst of the tug-of-war between those who doggedly insisted that politics has no place in an international scientific congress and those who were equally insistent that, whether one liked it or not, politics permeated the Moscow congress's organization, proceedings, and implications, occasions for potential disaster severely challenged IPSA's decisionmakers:

1. Had the proposed boycott by U.S. political scientists taken place, it might well have split the association itself.

2. Had the Israeli visas failed to arrive in time—and they literally reached the participants only hours before they were scheduled to leave for Moscow—IPSA's executive committee would doubtless have honored its commitment even on very short notice to cancel the congress.

3. Had bona fide political scientists from South Africa or Taiwan[4] registered for the congress, Soviet authorities might well have balked at issuing visas; and, while this would not have been a violation of IPSA's resolution of August 1978 (since neither country was a collective member of the association), it could have reopened the question of Soviet good faith.

4. Had the IPSA leadership insisted that a well-known Soviet dissident be permitted to address a working session and the Soviets persisted in denying him access to the halls of Moscow State University, where the congress was held, the effect would have been chilling.

5. Had any of the participants initiated a politically motivated demonstration in an IPSA session or elsewhere, or had the Soviet police been less lax about permitting participants to visit Soviet dissidents in their homes, untoward confrontations might have resulted.[5]

All these events were at one time or another very real possibilities. That they did not occur was due to the desire of Soviet authorities, IPSA officers, and the participants themselves to hold a "normal" scientific congress in Moscow. The Olympics of 1980 and 1984 nonetheless indicate that circumstances can change. It is quite likely, for instance, that an IPSA world congress in Moscow scheduled for 1980, that is, after the crisis in Afghanistan, would have collapsed entirely or at least in large part. It is just as likely that political considerations will affect participation in future IPSA congresses.

As new national associations join IPSA, and as an international ethic calling for a redistribution of the world's resources (including scientific information) grows, issues of national pride and international equity become increasingly important. A main argument for holding the congresses of 1979 and 1982 in the Soviet Union and Brazil, respectively, was to recognize the contribution made to international political science by these two countries. We may expect political scientists in still other countries not yet tapped for world congresses to feel that their own countries should be considered soon.

The issue of equity raises some implications for IPSA's future. On the one hand, to the extent that the argument in favor of distributing world congresses equitably runs counter to IPSA's need to have an invitation with financial guarantees from a national association, the prospect is for a serious reconsideration of the nature and organization of world congresses. On the other hand, the association may be able to deal with this problem by ensuring that its meetings between the triennial world congresses are distributed more evenly among the member associations. While this is possible for meetings of the IPSA executive committee, it may not be so for its research committees and study groups, the membership of which is normally not evenly distributed in this way.

These lines of argument point to one central fact: The political functionality of world congresses, albeit marginal to date, lies only slightly below the surface in any international scientific setting. The selection by an international scientific association of a site for an international meeting is essentially a political process. And so are such matters as the behavior of groups with points to prove no less than government attitudes toward ISCs held on their own soil or elsewhere. These are political processes that deserve further analytic attention.

Notes

1. This calculation rests on a general division of responses into political, scientific, and personal categories; respondents did not cite disciplinary reasons for going or not going to Moscow.

2. To be clear, we must add that one might believe that one's presence could have a political impact but not mention this as a reason for going to Moscow. Similarly, respondents might give political reasons for not going (e.g., as a matter of personal political ethics) without believing that their presence or absence would have any political impact on the Soviet Union.

3. A different way of looking at Table 5.5 would note that, of the total of 398 comments on both the "best" and "worst" panels, only 31 (8%) specifically criticized Soviet behavior.

4. At least one South African political scientist expressed interest in participating in a session at Moscow, but evidently did not follow up on the idea; and, in the week before the congress was to convene, a representative of Taiwan's Chinese Political Science Association telegraphed a U.S. scholar to regret that it was unable to send a delegate to Moscow, "owing delay of secretariat in issuing registration certificate." For a similar problem faced in 1986 with respect to the World Congress of Archeologists, see Walker (1986).

5. The only untoward incident known to us that involved an IPSA participant occurred on the day after the congress closed. A Canadian lawyer

and professor of law, who reports having gone to Moscow because it afforded him an otherwise unavailable opportunity to meet with Soviet dissident scientists and to present their case to Soviet officials, apparently violated Soviet law by journeying without formal permission beyond the city limits of Moscow; 3 hours after his arrest the police placed him on a flight to Canada (Giniger, 1979). Other congress participants who stayed on in the Soviet Union reported that official tolerance toward visits to dissidents ceased, sometimes rather abruptly, when the congress ended.

SIX
Functions of International Scientific Congresses

For close to four decades the International Political Science Association has sponsored triennial world congresses in the belief that they help political scientists meet certain goals. The prospect for the future is that IPSA will continue to organize such congresses. Our survey of political scientists, besides telling us something about those who did and those who did not attend the IPSA world congress of 1979, explains why they went to Moscow and the functions they see these meetings serving. In the data are implications for how the association might better plan for future world congresses and, more generally, how it might help political scientists to communicate internationally. This chapter outlines what we see as the key functions of international scientific congresses before turning to some suggestions for enhancing their usefulness.

Individual Political Scientists

Participants as a Scientific Elite

The comparative data on North American political scientists show clearly that participants in IPSA world congresses form part of the discipline's leading stratum. Compared to those who did not sign up to attend IPSA's world congress in Moscow, registrants have stronger records of scholarly activity, are more adept internationally, and enjoy higher professional status.

This fact is not surprising given that, in any academic discipline, activity and status generally reinforce each other. In this sense, international scientific congresses are merely another arena in which scientists can be active. Those who participate typically have histories of thriving on activity, and we might well suspect that they consciously seek out appropriate arenas.

Participants thus constitute a self-selected group. Scientists with other goals evidently decide not to spend their resources in attending ISCs or, as in the case of a substantial number of the nonregistrants surveyed here, are simply not alert to the fact that such meetings take place.

An international scientific association's procedure for choosing congress participants fundamentally reinforces the principle of self-selection. However broadly congress organizers cast their nets, they lean toward individuals with records of achievement or newer members of the profession whose promise is certified by those already enjoying status. Two aspects of the process of developing ISC programs—far from unique to the International Political Science Association—are germane here:

1. A strong emphasis on multinational participation means the possibility that the person organizing a session is not completely familiar with all scientists throughout the world who are conducting significant research on the specified topic. A simple rule of thumb in such circumstances is to fill the session with highly visible scientists known to the organizer or else younger scientists whom more visible colleagues recommend.

2. An alternative procedure would require the scientist seeking to make a presentation to submit a full-fledged paper that the organizer (or review panel) could then examine for quality. The constraints of time and exigencies of the worldwide communications system being what they are, this procedure is less practicable than it might be for a national association. The result is the temptation to accept and review not finished papers but abstracts, which usually turn out to be statements of intent rather than concise summaries of research completed.

Actual practice usually combines the two procedures. It thus sustains the existing network of scientists (and their likely heirs) while keeping open to outsiders who submit interesting proposals the possibility of membership in the network.

Rewards

Why do accomplished scientists want to attend world congresses? The obvious answer is that they find participation rewarding.[1] Phrased somewhat differently, from the individual scientist's vantage point, a key function of ISCs is to provide rewards. Now, then, what are these rewards? Chapter 3 revealed that our respondents identify them primarily in terms of *direct scientific communication* (Table 3.5).[2] Of signal importance are developing and maintaining contacts with other productive scientists (cited by 32 percent of the registrants), general scientific communication (22%), keeping up with new work, developments, and approaches (13%), and broadening intellectual, disciplinary, and international perspectives (13%). Chapter 4 added that, of the political scientists reporting some major modification in their work as a result of attending the Moscow meetings,[3] about one in three traces it to either the written papers (40%), their presentation (35%), and/or discussion in scheduled sessions (33%)—together accounting for three in five of the responses given.

If, however, direct scientific communication is the sole reward offered those considering whether or not they should invest their time and other resources in attending an ISC, then we (and, presumably, the scientists themselves) must ask whether or not the congress produces the greatest benefit for the costs incurred. It probably does not. Expanded publishing and abstracting services, electronic mail, teleconferencing, and even the telephone would go far toward providing a more cost-effective functional equivalent. Scientists with specific questions on their minds would doubtless find attending an ICS an expensive way to secure answers.

But in fact, as our capabilities for these other modes of scientific communication grow, the triennial world congress of political science seems to be ever more important. It attracts an increasing number of both participants and requests to hold sessions. This suggests that the lack of creative thinking on the part of political scientists is not at fault for failing to find functional equivalents for world congresses, but rather that ISCs provide other, perhaps less easily identifiable rewards.

One such reward is *serendipitous learning*. Bernard Barber (1968: 98) points to the "interesting suggestion" stemming from general sociological ideas and Menzel's (1959) research that scientists "sometimes think in terms of too rational a conception of the communication process; that is, they may be expecting too much from the journals and the formal meetings." Excessively goal-directed behavior can actually be dysfunctional for scientific learning. Participants who fill every minute with sessions to attend and papers to read, while leaving little time free for informal interaction with colleagues, may not be making the best use of the learning opportunities the congress affords them. By the same token, congress organizers who overschedule participants may not be doing them a favor.

This is not to say that such approaches to ISCs are useless. Presenting and listening to papers are important links in the transmission belt of scientific communication. But overscheduling may restrict participants' ability to be receptive to information the importance of which is not immediately apparent. "Scientists cannot always know precisely what they want and merely push a computer button to get it," Barber (1968: 98) points out. "Often, through 'milling around' at meetings, through chance visits, through indirect channels, they get essential information which they can recognize as essential only when they get it." Informal, unplanned communication at ISCs broadens access to a significant international network of political scientists—a network of like-minded individuals with whom an active scientist can talk about current developments, try out new ideas, scout for collaborators in future research, and sniff in the wind for research areas likely to break open in the near future.

Now, scientists do not go to an international congress with the explicit intent to learn serendipitously. Formal opportunities for exchanges of information doubtless dominate their planning—as they certainly do the calculations of administrators who must approve and/or fund the participants' travel requests. Nevertheless, their past experience tells many scientists that a certain probability of serendipitous learning exists.[4] It is the possibility of its reoccurrence that lends vitality to the very idea of attending the congress, and participants may promise themselves to be responsive should they encounter it again.

Related to and in fact enhancing serendipitous learning are the travel, conviviality, and other rewards classified in Chapter 1 under the rubric "personal enrichment." Although the typical respondent filling out a questionnaire received in the mail doubtless plays down the importance of such considerations, possibly in the belief that they may seem less "noble" than scientific communication, our feeling is that, used intelligently, these opportunities constitute an important element of the ambience that invigorates scientific communication. Sharing a pot of coffee at a riverside café or quiet dinner at a good restaurant may well provide scientists with the best occasion for hashing out different conceptualizations or outlining ways to solve a particular puzzle. Lodge's (1984: 238) biting observation—"afterwards, when they are back home, and friends and family ask if they enjoyed the conference, they say, oh yes, but not so much for the papers, which were pretty boring, as for the informal contacts one makes on these occasions"—points to an essential truth. The informal contacts *are* important.

Herein lies a key latent function of international scientific congresses. An ISC structured to facilitate informal communication, besides making serendipitous learning more likely, enhances the contextual framework in which participants seek to understand the scientific information communicated through more formal channels. *Informal communication makes formal communication in ISCs sensible.* Stripped of opportunities for informal communication, congresses are surely less cost-efficient for individual participants than are other means for exchanging information. Informal interaction helps scientists to catch nuances, clear up ambiguities, evaluate the depth and breadth of other scientists, and pursue substantive points until there is, if not agreement, then at least mutual understanding of where differences lie. Although perhaps only poorly articulated by participants, this latent function greases the skids for effective scientific communication.

International scientific congresses perform a second latent function for individual participants. *Their selection procedures confirm individual scientists as accepted (or candidate) members of an international disciplinary elite.* This has a double impact. In the short run, as we have already noted, ISCs reward the active by making it *ceteris paribus* easier for them to obtain places on the program. With invitations in hand, they can approach funding sources, make travel plans, and begin to anticipate some of the other rewards accruing to ISC participants. All this may boost the scientists' egos and lend prestige, both at home and abroad, to their work. Such considerations apparently undergird the desire for scientific communication as the immediate reasons leading scientists attend international scientific congresses.

More interesting is a second, long-range impact: Although scientists may not be aware of it at the time, successful participation in an ISC gives them a claim on the future. For one thing, such participation makes it more likely that they will be asked to join in the next congress and in myriad other activities spinning off from the international association's scientific program. For another thing, successful participation in a congress gives scientists a firmer basis for taking an active role in the international association itself. How scientists react to this associational recognition that they are members of the international disciplinary elite may vary widely, of course. Some will see it merely as another accolade, as confirmation of a status they always knew they deserved. Others will see it as an instrument to accomplish other goals, such as a broadened research agenda or international scientific organizational activity.

Still another latent function of the international scientific congress vis-à-vis participants pertains to their research. *ISCs help set individual research agendas.* IPSA world congresses unabashedly cater to research-oriented political scientists. Its process of selecting papergivers and discussants, we suggested earlier, gives great weight to those who have achieved a name for themselves through their research. Not surprisingly, then, over four-fifths of our respondents who registered to attend the Moscow meetings identify themselves as primarily researchers rather than teachers or administrators.[5] And, of those reporting a significant impact on their work activity, almost three in four (73%) specify research or publications as the type of activity modified while only a fifth (21%) cite teaching.[6] To be sure, we might assume that the confrontation of participants at the international congress with an array of diverse perspectives would stimulate some rethinking about the discipline itself and how it should be presented to students. The point is more that the selection process and the climate at the meetings strongly encourage a preference for research.

What is more, by selecting participants who focus on certain kinds of issues or work with particular paradigms, the ISC "certifies" the centrality of what they are doing. The effect is to tell scientists what kind of research is most likely to earn them a place on the program of the next world congress. Those doing something different have several options. They can change directions, live with the low likelihood of being invited to attend world congresses, or try to participate anyway, in the knowledge that theirs will be voices in the wilderness. Another alternative is to seek to influence the international scientific association's process for making decisions about the content of and participation in future sessions. Given the fundamental inertia of such associations, however, the last row would be a tough one to hoe.

Research Organizations

Our research design did not permit us to delve into the functionality of ISCs for the university, governmental agency, laboratory, or research institute sending scientists as participants. Chapter 1 suggested that such a research organization stands to benefit from ISCs in various ways: making the scientists it employs happier by according them opportunities for communication and travel, acquiring some part of the information these scientists obtain at the meetings, gaining the organization recognition for its research program and personnel, and attracting potential recruits. All these may augment the research organization's effectiveness and reputation. Although open-ended items on our questionnaire provided opportunities for respondents to volunteer pertinent views, in fact none did so. Research specifically designed to address this issue might survey both scientists and administrators at a sample of research organizations, and trace through (for example, by analyzing citations) the concrete impact attending an ISC has on the organization's published work. Such research could contribute significantly to our understanding of the role of international scientific congresses in advancing knowledge.

Scientific Associations

Chapter 2 noted our expectation that political scientists filling out the questionnaires would not be especially alert to the functionality of international scientific congresses for disciplinary associations *qua* associations. Only a few, we felt, would have sufficient knowledge about the activities and needs of their national association or IPSA to provide anything more than guesses about the associational impact of the Moscow meetings. This assessment turned out to be accurate. Asked about the chief functions of ISCs for the political science profession (Table 3.5), more than twice as many registrants (63%) emphasized the exchange of information and other scientific values as those who cited the entire range of disciplinary values:

enhancing the prestige of the discipline, creating a sense of professional identity, or institutionalization (11%); broadening the discipline's international dimensions or reducing parochial perspectives (10%); and improving the quality of political science, assessing the state of the art, or identifying new trends (9%).

International Institutionalization

And yet, reading between the lines of such findings, and taking into account the variety of issues that arose in organizing and carrying out the Moscow meetings, we find at the international level a number of associational functions meriting attention. The most obvious of these derives from the fact that the congress actually took place. IPSA issued a call for a world congress to be held in the Soviet Union and answering it were political scientists from around the world, including a substantial number from a country where some disciplinary leaders urged their colleagues to boycott the meetings. IPSA's organizing committees absolutely refused to permit political considerations to impede their progress; and individual scientists attending the meetings refused to be put off the track by what some saw as the intrusion of cold-war politics into the proceedings. The association thus met head-on and weathered the disruptive storm posed by a politicized environment.

Another potentially disruptive storm raised by the Moscow meetings forced the association to re-examine its intellectual and organizational priorities. IPSA had traditionally focused on North American and Western European concerns. To be sure, from its earliest years the association included collective and individual members from socialist countries and the Third World, its governing bodies embraced their representatives, and from time to time IPSA-sponsored roundtables met in those parts of the world. However, viewed in the framework of IPSA's overall activities, such countries were peripheral to the association's main thrust. Holding a world congress in Moscow meant that IPSA had to face its worldwide responsibilities. It had to come to terms with the possibility that scientists with non-Western perspectives would dominate the proceedings, and it had to deal seriously with such matters as blocked currencies, travel restrictions, limited access to reproduction equipment, and the like.[7] That it did so fairly effectively again indicates that IPSA had come of age internationally.[8]

However we measure its success, then, *the minimal fact that the congress took place without major incident bolstered substantially the disciplinary standing of the International Political Science Association*. The association's ability to master significant problems, if not to resolve them permanently, merely enhanced its authority. Faced with challenges to the association's control over its own meetings, the bulk of political scientists from at least nonsocialist countries identified themselves with the association, its aims, and its policies. And, of course, the icing on the cake was the fact that participants rated the congress highly successful in other regards. By far the majority went home feeling positive about effective scientific communication, fruitful contacts, lively interchanges, and so forth. If any doubt existed before 1979 that IPSA was an effective international scientific association with a global scope, the Moscow meetings put that doubt to rest.

Reward Structure

We spoke earlier of the functionality of international scientific congresses in providing manifest and latent rewards for individual participants. Through their programmatic decisions those organizing ISCs accord recognition to certain lines of research, confer status on individual researchers, and enhance the latter's access to the international disciplinary elite. The way in which such decisions are made and the rationale used to justify them constitute the international scientific association's reward structure. From the vantage point of the individual, the most important outcome of an ISC's reward structure may be the degree to which it reinforces the discipline's more general reward structure, that is, makes it more likely that activities meriting praise today will also do so tomorrow, that those enjoying high status today will continue to enjoy it tomorrow. What is important from the vantage point of the international association is *its ability to implement a reward structure* that individual scientists and national associations accept as legitimate. This in turn *contributes to the legitimacy of the international association.*

This latent function has identifiable consequences. First, to the extent that it strengthens the often inchoate cycle of professional activity and rewards, it clarifies that cycle, that is, makes it clearer what criteria are to be used in judging contributions, no less than who belongs to the international disciplinary elite and who does not. Such clarification can be functional for the association by making it easier for program organizers to identify and invite the discipline's leading stratum to participate in future ISCs. The participation of these disciplinary leaders in turn lends the meetings an added cachet of respectability, which then makes it more possible for the association to attract other participants and perhaps even to raise funds for travel and other purposes. Carried to an extreme, however, this self-reinforcing cycle could lead to an international disciplinary class structure that could doom the association to the dustbin of history.

Second, an international associational reward structure lends a degree of stability to the international scientific association itself. Whether this is good or bad depends on the use to which the association's officers put the stabilizing influence. They could use it as a basis on which to expand the association's services to and impact on the discipline—for example, redoubling efforts to raise travel funds for Third World participants, or encouraging the development of political science in countries where it is now weak or absent. Alternatively, they could capitalize on the stabilizing influence by providing more perquisites (such as increased international travel) for themselves and/or new staff and buildings for the association.

Related to these consequences is a third one linked to the discipline's future. A stable international reward structure gives the association controlling it substantial influence over the process of recruiting and socializing younger scientists. It tells them (and their employers) that an important path toward accomplishing their goals—access to key international communication networks, high professional status, and so forth—runs through the association and its activities, including congresses. Such a message will also implant in the minds of these younger scholars the scientific and other norms (for example, a strong orientation toward research) of the international disciplinary elite that makes decisions about participation. The negative side of this control is the possibility that the latter will seek merely to reproduce scientists like themselves, thereby diminishing the chances for intellectual innovation or upward mobility on the part of those who do not fit today's molds.

Political Functions

National Societies

The functionality of international scientific congresses for national societies, as represented by their governments, does not loom large in our respondents' imagery. They are aware that the country hosting such a congress may benefit in the form of the attention it receives, enhancement of its scientific establishment, or tourist revenues. They nevertheless consider these gains less important than what individual scientists and the scientific discipline take away from ISCs. Least of all do they see such benefits as contributing much to the state's international power position.

The argument that ISCs are available instruments that can or should be used for larger political purposes also carries little weight. In principle, states (or their citizens on governing councils of international scientific associations) could dangle before a country they wish to influence the prospect of locating an ISC within its borders. Few of our respondents commenting on this possibility, however, seem to feel that a country of the magnitude of the Soviet Union or indeed any other state that has hosted an IPSA world congress would rise to such bait. At best, a substantial minority expresses the view that, by participating in an ISC in a closed society, scientists might be able to aid those in the country seeking its opening.

In short, the data surveyed in this book make it clear that political scientists—and, by implication, other scientists as well—believe that political considerations should not be permitted to intrude into their scientific congresses. The problem is that sometimes they can hardly escape such intrusions. Selecting a site for a world congress may tempt national associations or their governments to take essentially political stances for or against a potential host country. It may be just as difficult to ignore individual scientists who, for their own reasons or acting on behalf of groups with which they identify, wish to make a political fuss. Then, too, IPSA can do little to prevent host countries from trying to turn congresses to their own advantage. Judging from their comments, however, participants feel that such actions, however irritating they may be, have little immediate impact.

Circumstances will determine whether or not such incidents have a broader impact. In a time of "normal" international discourse, when states have no particular axes to grind and subnational groups are not trying to make a point, none of the above incidents would make large waves. An international scientific association could rely on the disinclination of governments to block its activities, and on the intervention of national disciplinary leaders to persuade recalcitrant bureaucrats and political-minded colleagues to adopt a more expansive attitude. In a time of trouble, by contrast, states and their citizens may forget or ignore the earlier argument that freedom of scientific communication serves their own long-range interests. Partisan uproar focusing on some ISC is thus more an effect than a cause of general political turmoil.

International Systemic Structure

The political use of international scientific congresses is in this sense a function of the structure of the international system. Scientists themselves—if we may judge from the claims made by those from nonsocialist countries who attended the IPSA world congress in Moscow—generally adhere to the oft-postulated norm of scientific communalism (Merton, 1942): an "institutional conception of science as part of the public domain . . . linked with the imperative for communication of findings." At least some of them are nevertheless prepared to swing into line behind their governments when the structure of the international system changes.

The international system obtaining in 1976-1979 was one characterized by the efforts of the superpowers and their allies to achieve East-West détente. Accordingly, the main international actors were emphasizing cooperative endeavors and exchanges of all sorts. International scientific congresses bringing together scientists from all parts of the world were natural in such a climate. Government policy thus reinforced the scientists' more general proclivity toward "full and open communication" (Merton, 1942). Only a few political scientists, most but not all of them in the United States, felt that Soviet violations of human rights (in this case, the rights of dissident scientists) were a sufficiently serious breach of faith that they warranted retaliation in the form of a boycott.

Our data do not reveal how the nonsocialist community of political scientists would have responded to a changed international system. How many of them would have changed sides on the question of full and open communication? Evidence from other scientific fields after the Soviet incursion into Afghanistan suggests that a substantial number in a handful of countries would have expressed strong reservations about continued scientific cooperation with the Soviet Union and even cancelled their planned participation in congresses being held in that country. The half-life of such protests in the early 1980s nevertheless proved to be short and by now exchange programs broken off a half-decade ago are being resumed.[9]

Functional Theories of Integration

In the theories of some writers (e.g. Angell, 1969, 1981), success in internationalizing science will expand the web of international interdependence in ways that contribute to peaceful relations among nation-states. In such theories the functions of international scientific congresses are to promote international understanding and to encourage international networks among scientists. The burden of the argument, of course, is not solely on international science. It is but one strand in the putative web of interdependence. International science is nevertheless a crucial strand because of its symbolic significance for world order and because success in this area may well spill over into other fields of human activity.

Our survey does not provide conclusive proof on the validity of these points. Some networking did emerge from the Moscow meetings. Substantial numbers of registrants justified the Moscow world congress in terms of reducing parochialism at both the individual and disciplinary levels. And, although we included no items specifically on this point, respondents occasionally volunteered the view that the IPSA congress had a positive impact on international relations. Consider, for example, the question of whether or not IPSA's original decision to hold the world congress in Moscow was correct. Three in ten (29%) of the responses by those who approved it gave reasons referring to promoting positive international relations. Our hunch is that more specific questions would have yielded considerable acceptance of the proposition that international science promotes world order.

But can we be sure about this? Certainly the evidence regarding changes in the participants' views of the Soviet governmental apparatus does not suggest that familiarity breeds admiration or even acceptance. What effect an enhanced understanding of the circumstances of the Soviet people will have in the long run is a question our data cannot answer. This kind of evidence is nevertheless beside the point. The more important question is the extent to which fruitful interaction among scientists can produce an international scientific culture that influences policymakers to mitigate conflicts and strengthen transnational political ties. The proof of the pudding lies in part in the extent to which political scientists attending ISCs pick up an "international" perspective on political matters, carry it over into their research and classroom instruction, and conduct future exchanges with foreign scholars they meet at these congresses. The other part of the proof requires some indication of how policymakers might deal with such an international scientific culture.

Structure and Change in the International System

Of particular interest to students of international social change is the issue of how international scientific congresses influence the distribution of such scientific values as skill, knowledge, and rewards. ISCs in any field have the potential for transferring such disciplinary values from the "have" to the "have-not" states. The questions of concern are whether transfers actually take place, the extent to which transfers leave the "have-not" states in a position of greater autonomy vs. dependency, and the degree of seriousness with which the "have" states take into account the concerns and special needs of the others.

As far as scientific growth in the Third World is concerned, our data and more general analysis indicate that international political scientific congresses may be performing quite unevenly the function of transferring disciplinary values. First, their reward structure as outlined earlier places strong emphasis on highly visible scientists, most of whom work in a traditionally Western mode of analysis. Save for token representatives, participants selected from Third World countries tend to be those who have studied in the West and/or use predominantly Western paradigms—with both categories quite heavily relying on and citing the Western scientific literature. The exception to this generalization is the unusually large number of scientists from Latin America who presented papers at the Rio de Janeiro meetings 1982. Latin American participation nevertheless dropped off at the Paris meetings of 1985. This fact reinforces the argument made earlier that, at least until the problem of high transportation costs can be resolved, a regular rotation of sites provides an important means for transferring disciplinary values.

Second, at the Moscow world congress, Third World participants were fairly isolated. They indicate in response to our questionnaire that they were reasonably active in seeking informal contacts at the congress itself albeit less so in trying to maintain them afterwards. Participants from North America and other Western countries, though, put their Third World colleagues at the bottom of the list when it came to subsequent networking. At the same time, the Third World scientists report a substantially greater-than-average degree of modification in their work activities as a result of attending the congress. In a way, these scientists ended up playing a role more as recipients of information about substance and techniques than as active contributors to the scientific endeavor.[10]

The complex of problems implicit in an international scientific congress's functionality for redistributing scientific values on a worldwide basis is one that for some time to come will arrest the attention of IPSA's leadership and the organizers of its future world congresses. Available evidence does not suggest that the Moscow world congress did much to redress the disciplinary imbalance between North and South; nor are there clear guidelines about how this task could be accomplished and, in fact, whether or not the ISC is an appropriate instrument to that end. The International Political Science Association's critics sometimes complain that it is not taking the issue seriously enough. Others, however, have argued that structural conditions in the Third World (such as governmental distrust of political science as a discipline and the lack of funds for research) have prevented more rapid movement and that, indeed, the excursions to Moscow in 1979 and to Rio de Janeiro in 1982 moved the association too far from the central disciplinary concerns of political science.

Transferring disciplinary values between East and West is quite another matter. With a few exceptions, the political scientists from socialist countries who have been most successful in the international disciplinary framework have been those able to work in a Marxist tradition but sufficiently flexible in their thinking to communicate effectively with Western political scientists working in a non-Marxist tradition. The unusually large number of Soviet and East European scientists at the Moscow meetings (610 registrants) provided the first large-scale test of the proposition that East-West communication in political science is possible. The results were moderately positive, as we saw in Chapter 4. Some irritation about what they saw as their socialist colleagues' formalistic pronouncements in scheduled sessions notwithstanding, our nonsocialist respondents generally found the opportunities for informal contacts useful, and many sought to extend the contacts beyond the Moscow meetings. As the desert fox told Antoine de Saint Exupéry's little prince, building the mutual trust required for effective communication takes a while. Holding more meetings in Eastern Europe may facilitate such communication even if it does not produce a perfect meeting of minds on disciplinary values.

Some Future Directions

The data surveyed in this book point to several general conclusions regarding international scientific congresses in general and IPSA world congresses in particular. First, an ISC clearly serves several valuable functions for various members of a scientific consocation. But, and this is the second point, its ability to perform these functions is quite uneven. The typical ISC is better, for instance, at giving individuals opportunities for scientific communication than at trying to effect some political outcome.

Third, many of these functions are quite straightforward, there for all to see. Sessions at which scientists present their ideas and findings permit participants from around the world to learn about research under way in countries and intellectual settings other than their own, obtain feedback on their own work, and exchange information. Similarly, the international scientific association that organizes an ISC performs an obvious service for the profession. An IPSA world congress is an intellectual watering place for current and future members of the discipline's leading stratum, and a framework for developing international networks of scientists seeking to advance knowledge in some particular subfield.

Fourth, other functions are less apparent to casual observers and even participants. What is more, the ability of an international scientific congress to perform key latent functions goes far toward explaining its success with respect to more manifest functions. The free use of unorganized and sometimes recondite informal channels gives formally communicated information a context that makes it more meaningful to working scientists. In some ways an ISC's formal sessions are only a pretext that enables scientists to get together informally to discuss what affects them most directly. By the same token, IPSA's success in mounting a world congress strengthens its hold over the international scientific consocation we call political science. The disciplinary integration an ISC enhances redounds to the benefit of the international scientific association; and this in turn gives the association a firmer basis to develop further congresses and other activities that serve the discipline. Latent functions such as these drive the entire scientific communication process.

Possibilities nonetheless exist, we feel, for improving the ability of IPSA world congresses to carry out their multifarious functions. The following pages outline some possibilities aimed particularly at improving scientific communication and contributing to the growth of an international science of politics. A few suggestions require only minor modifications in standard operating procedures. Achieving other goals, however, may require a fundamental rethinking of the nature and organization of international scientific congresses.

Quality of IPSA World Congresses

Comments offered by our respondents indicate that IPSA world congresses have room for improvement. Some ideas along this line are essentially technical—the need for a professional on the IPSA staff to assist in organizing the world congresses; ways to structure the program and program committee, distribute papers, exhibit books, and schedule panels; expanded facilities for simultaneous translation—and need not concern us here. More interesting are those that go to the heart of an ISC as a medium for scientific communication.

One is the obvious point that national and international political considerations must not be permitted to intrude into the process of setting up and running a world congress. This concern is of course not peculiar to political science. At the more general level the International Council of Scientific Unions has spent considerable time seeking to realize the "well-established agreement that scientific meetings shall not be disturbed by political statements or by activities of a political nature."[11] IPSA, too, as we have seen, has developed procedures to minimize the possibility of political intrusions. These procedures proved to be reasonably effective during the Moscow world congress of 1979 and afterwards. But each world congress is a new test, and that to be held in August 1988 in Washington, D.C. is no exception.

Second, the scientific credibility of the IPSA world congress requires greater attention to quality controls. The tendency of organizers to emphasize balanced representation of papergivers by region rather than by the quality of their papers portends problems for the future. Though it is nowhere spelled out as such in IPSA documentation, the "ideal" panel set up by the program committee contains one papergiver each from North America, other Western countries, the socialist countries, and the Third World. Frequently this means turning down an interesting paper because that region's "quota" has already been reached, or accepting a weak paper because the panel lacks a "representative" of a particular region. The general practice of accepting for the program titles of papers rather than finished papers exacerbates this situation. In short, quality controls are rudimentary and applied at best unevenly.[12]

While such policies may serve an institutional goal, namely, broadening IPSA's membership and participation in its world congresses, they also entail a cost. If active scientists attend too many panels put together on some basis other than the quality of the research to be presented, then they may well lose interest in both the congresses and the association sponsoring them. It is precisely this loss of topflight scientists that *no* international scientific association can afford. Alternatively, such scientists may begin to ignore the prestigious, representative sessions to focus instead on the activities of smaller working groups either contained within the association or meeting concurrently with it. It is this alternative that suggests an important consideration for future IPSA world congresses, networking, to which we shall return later.

A third task is far more complex: ensuring the internationality of world congresses. Internationality means more than simply assembling participants from all over the world. It implies significant interaction among them. If nonscientific boundaries had no meaning, then we would expect networks emerging within some part of the discipline to be completely random in terms of the geographic distribution of their members.[13] Our study suggests that this is far from true today. Only in part can we attribute the salience of national boundaries to IPSA's federal structure, an association of national associations, with which each of its own members identify. More importantly, significant scientific discontinuities reinforce these national boundaries. If it is true, as the data indicate, that Western scientists slight networking opportunities with colleagues from the Third World, then the explanation surely lies less in national and other prejudices than in these scientists' tendency to avoid interaction with those whom they consider less substantively or methodologically proficient than themselves.

How can such nonscientific barriers to internationality be broken down? Easy answers are not at hand. Still, one point seems certain: More careful selection of participants rather than lowered quality controls is imperative. A Third World country might benefit most in the long run by sending its best scientists, even though they are not in tune with generally prevailing paradigms and approaches and even though they have language difficulties. Such a step would pose new tasks. For one thing, the international association would have to deal seriously with a polyglot world rather than assuming that all participants are thoroughly conversant in English and/or French. An increased demand for simultaneous translation services would in turn raise the financial cost of holding a world congress. For another thing, scholars from Western countries must be prepared to enter into dialogues in which they listen as well as talk. This is a matter of recruitment: searching out scientists who can contribute to and learn from a genuinely two-way dialogue. It also requires the ISC to give over program space to such focused—and, perhaps, risky—exchanges along with more traditional sessions at which papers are formally presented and discussed. This kind of restructuring is in its own way costly for an international scientific association.

Another way to strengthen IPSA's internationality is to broaden the geographic spread of potential sites for world congresses (and other meetings). The Moscow meeting greatly increased participation by East Europeans and the Rio meeting that followed attracted many Latin Americans. It stands to reason that, even if these upsurges in activity are not sustained as the congress site moves elsewhere, some portion of the newly won participants will maintain their ties with the association. Then why not simply institute a firm principle of rotating sites? Whatever support it finds among IPSA's leaders and our respondents, the principle raises sharply the question of financing.

Finances and World Congress Sites

The sensitivity of decisions about sites for IPSA world congresses argues for more attention to the way in which these decisions are made. A fundamental revision in procedures is clearly more easily proposed than accomplished. As it is now, IPSA's emphasis on voluntarism forces it to rely on a national association willing to undertake the organizational work and raise the necessary funds. These funds turn out to be vital. Thus the French government provided a grant of $150,000 to help finance the Paris meetings in 1985. And yet, if we take into account the real costs of an IPSA world congress (including the travel and per diem of participants), then we realize that this sum probably represents no more than 5 percent of the total outlay in 1985.[14] The effect of relying on this procedure is that the tail wags the dog.

Recognizing the financial straits in which doubtless all international scientific associations find themselves, and IPSA is certainly no exception, it may seem gratuitous to recommend searching for the means to divorce decisions about sites from financial considerations. A modicum of financial independence (or some other solution, such as greater self-financing of world congresses[15]) can nevertheless enable IPSA to seek an appropriate site rather than vice versa. One useful model is a congress site that does not offer external participants too many nonscholarly distractions or indigenous participants the opportunity to carry on their normal teaching or administrative responsibilities while the congress is in session. This may mean a single conference facility that can house 2,000 to 3,000 people, one far enough away from major cities that participants can keep their minds on the business at hand and yet close enough to attractive touristic or cultural sites that organized or informal visits can be arranged on a free afternoon and evening. Such an environment of limited mobility would strongly increase the opportunities for informal discussions and networking.

Informal Networking

What comes up time and again in our analysis is the importance of informal modes of communication. They seem to produce the greatest amount of learning, a sense of empathy with scholars working in other countries under other conditions, and possibly even a feeling that an international political science community exists, however circumscribed by political conditions and communication barriers it may be. A major task of an international scientific congress, or, indeed, any scientific congress, may well be to create a framework in which informal networks (or "invisible colleges") can emerge and thrive. The preparation of papers for presentation at formal congress sessions may serve other purposes (such as committing scholars to putting their thoughts down on paper). In this context, they nevertheless serve more than anything else as a device for helping scientists to identify others with similar interests, suggesting topics for informal discussions, and, more generally, legitimating the opportunities for informal networks of scholars to operate effectively.

IPSA's mushrooming number of research committees and study groups testifies to the importance of networking for political scientists. To meet the association's conditions, a research committee must include on its governing committee persons from at least a half dozen countries, provide some medium for exchange of information, and hold occasional conferences outside the congress setting. A research committee in good standing now has the right to organize two formal sessions at each IPSA world congress. (A study group becomes a research committee after it has functioned for several years and has organized an international congress for its members and others; upon request, it is accorded the privilege of setting up one formal session at the world congress.) Research committees and study groups raise their own funds, sometimes with the IPSA secretariat's assistance, and determine their own procedures. They thus have greater freedom of action than the parent body in such matters as selecting sites for meetings, and inviting participants on the basis of their scientific merit rather than merely for reasons of representativeness.

The research committees and study groups are rapidly becoming, at least in terms of scientific output, the most productive activity sponsored by IPSA. On the one hand, IPSA can enhance its overall effectiveness by encouraging the development and operation of these bodies. On the other hand, their centrifugal effect for IPSA as a whole cannot be ignored. Their increasing number means growing demands on the association for financial assistance, space in the program of the world congress, and a formal voice in IPSA's decisionmaking. The challenge facing the association is to accommodate the divergent interests of the research committees and study groups but at the same time maintaining some sense of what is central in the discipline of political science.

Another challenge for international scientific associations such as IPSA is to develop new and, one hopes, less cumbersome procedures for facilitating networking among scholars with related interests. Two ideas come to mind here. First, smaller workshops of individual networks may be one answer. Second, the rapid development of inexpensive facilities for computer networking makes it reasonable to explore Kochen's (1985: 299) idea of an "inquiring community," proposed to advance the use of social know-how in invention and innovation:

> Teams of social scientists, policy analysts, and policymakers would be structured both to take advantage of newer modes of communication and collective memory (computer conferencing), and to reduce the fear of making mistakes from which may come learning. Members could inject into the network a policy concern or proposed solution which others interested or with expertise in the issue could pick up. They could then pursue it in their own thinking and research, all the while remaining in constant contact with each other via teleconferencing, exchanging data, testing out ideas on relevant populations, and, more generally, seeking solutions to the policy problem.

To some measure groups of social scientists have already created mechanisms for such teleconferencing. It should be noted, however, that, even if access to the network is available to anyone interested in the subject matter, this kind of procedure for exchanging scientific information at least initially advantages scientists from developed countries where microprocessors are readily available. It may thus exacerbate the problem of "scientific dependency" that a number of writers have identified.

Workshops and teleconferencing, as well as IPSA's research committees and study groups, are most likely to work well within the framework provided by the association's more general world congresses. The ISC provides participants with a broad exposure to the discipline and hence a very different type of experience in communication and learning. It enables scientists to interact directly with specialists in a variety of subfields and from different scientific traditions. There is no substitute for face-to-face communication. In short, without the opportunities for cross-fertilization and recruitment of new members afforded by periodic world congresses, focused workshops and teleconferencing run the risk of self-encapsulation and decreasing relevance to the political science discipline as a whole. Developed appropriately, however, they hold out the promise of flexibility and significant scientific progress.

Diffusion of Research Paradigms and Results

Related to such measures is the need for IPSA to take a more active role in spreading research resources among its members. One problem of scientific communication is particularly acute. Although networking can ensure that experts on a particular topic share the latest paradigms and research results, and although annual meetings of national associations can keep generalists on top of other developments in their own countries, the 3-year gap between IPSA world congresses makes it difficult for political scientists to remain up-to-date on international research outside their own field of specialization. This is especially the case for scholars in countries without the resources to permit extensive travel or the purchase of books and journals from overseas. Moreover, insofar as some countries dominate the channels for scientific communication, the ideas of others are slow to gain attention. The long-term result may be the kind of "scientific dependency" that produces lopsided research and considerable resentment. The more immediate result is to entrench barriers to effective cross-national communication at IPSA world congresses.

To ease such problems, IPSA might develop occasional traveling seminars. By this we mean a team of scholars performing work at the forefront of some field within political science, and who are able to accept the invitation of countries or research institutes to conduct week-long seminars in their area of expertise. The goal would be two-way communication, that is, an exchange of information among peers rather than the creation of a master-pupil relationship. The visiting team would discuss its own research paradigms and results, but it would also listen carefully to those of its hosts.

Such traveling seminars could have a number of positive results.[16] First, if they are properly structured and carried out in good faith, learning will take place on both sides. Second, the resulting interaction may generate transcendent ideas to replace those deriving from more particularistic perspectives. The ideal is a political science of universal rather than merely parochial dimensions. Third, the seminars could spawn new networks of political scientists and expand existing ones. In this sense they would lay the groundwork for more effective communication at subsequent world congresses—two-way communication of the sort that will be required if the congresses are to be truly international.

A related project would aim at developing international data resources for research in political science. In recent years a number of teams have developed banks of reproducible data on political phenomena—public opinion, electoral behavior, civil strife, international wars and militarized disputes, trade and mail flows across national boundaries, and much more. In some areas, notably in North America and Western Europe, political scientists have set up inter-institutional consortia to clean, store, and disseminate such data. Enormous gaps in their coverage, both geographically and in terms of the types of data sets they include, nevertheless characterize these archives. By helping to expand the enterprise of collecting and archiving data, IPSA could greatly facilitate the exchange of scientific information and, again, better enable participants at world congresses to build on a common base of knowledge.

The experience of the meetings in Moscow, held in circumstances that maximized the potential for nonscientific disruption, demonstrates the importance of IPSA world congresses. Scientific communication triumphed in 1979. Some new ideas were generated, some networks developed. And, for the most part, the participants went home with a strong sense that the idea of an IPSA world congress is worthwhile. Room for improvement nevertheless exists; and it is possible for the International Political Science Association to undertake new activities that can greatly enhance the discipline's ability to communicate political science internationally.

Notes

1. We assume the scientists' rationality in the sense that they seek consciously to maximize their utilities. We thus ignore an entire range of questions dealing with unconscious behavior (e.g., the underlying motives that drive activity and hence the function activity serves for the personality).

2. Although respondents describe as their chief motive for attending ISCs the desire for scientific communication, their comments make it clear that personal circumstances—availability of funding, family commitments, timing, and convenience—are crucial in determining whether or not they in fact attend the meetings.

3. Almost a quarter (23%) of our respondents cite such a major modification; and surveys of psychologists and sociologists who participated in their world congresses of 1966 suggest that one-third may be the upper limit for such an explicitly recalled impact (Table 4.5). Although this is a modest result to show for the considerable time, energy, and money that many scholars put into the organization of ISCs, it may be more significant than it appears at first glance. Our question inquired about information that led to *major* changes only. It seems reasonable to assume that many more political scientists received information that was helpful or interesting but that did not fundamentally reorient their work. Then, too, scientists may well have received important new ideas in Moscow but were simply unable a year later to pinpoint their precise source. Something said in a corridor may not have struck home until many weeks or months later, and in a context that did not recall the original conversation.

4. Of the political scientists who report having significantly modified their work activities because of something they learned at the Moscow world congress (23 percent of the total), almost three-quarters (74%) cite as a source informal contacts; these constitute about two-fifths of the total responses given to this question (Table 4.5).

5. Thus 27 percent indicate that their interests are very heavily in research and another 53 percent that, while they are interested in both teaching and research, they lean toward the latter; by contrast, only one in seven

reports being mainly interested in teaching (2%) or leaning toward teaching (12%).

6. A study by the American Council on Education on the professional benefits to be derived from attending international scientific meetings supports this finding (Atelsek and Gomberg, 1981: 13). In a survey of department heads in the natural sciences at 760 colleges and universities in the United States, only 1 percent indicated that improvement in the quality of faculty teaching was the chief benefit of participation in these meetings.

7. Each of these matters led to protracted negotiations that yielded more or less adequate resolutions. In the case of participation, for instance, the Soviet organizing committee agreed to register no more than 500 scientists from socialist countries.

8. IPSA's Western vs. international focus continues to be a matter of concern in some quarters. We shall touch on these issues again.

9. The degree of governmental concern in such matters may well vary according to scientific field. Breaking off relations or maintaining secrecy in a technical area such as solid-state physics differs from similar steps in political science. From the vantage point of those who would limit the free flow of scientific information, barriers in the former aim at preventing the outflow of secret information useful for military and commercial purposes while barriers in the latter seek to keep out ideas that may contaminate domestic political discourse.

10. This consideration may explain in part the growing trend to hold international meetings in Third World countries (see Table 1.1).

11. This "Resolution on the Nonpolitical Tradition of ICSU," adopted in October 1966, appears in the Council's "Advice to Organizers of International Scientific Meetings" (ICSU, 1976).

12. Expressed in functional terms, the organ of a "living system" (cell, organism, organization) performing a particular function faces atrophy when it no longer can perform the function or when the function itself is replaced by another one (Miller, 1978: 83, 711). Accordingly, if we consider the formal session at a world congress to be important in its own right, and not just a fig leaf hiding an ISC's "true" (latent) function aimed at informal communication networks, then organizers must ensure that the formal session in fact performs the scientific communication function assigned to it. Attention to quality control is thus critical to maintaining the ISC as we know it today.

13. A complete model of interpersonal interaction would also take into account such variables as distance, the number of active scientists in each country, and diffusion rates of new knowledge.

14. As noted in the preface, we calculate the minimum real cost to be an average of $1,600 for each of the 1,763 participants, plus perhaps $150,000 for the costs of the program committee and related expenses; this amount, together with the $150,000 allocated to the French organizing committee (but eliminating double-counting), totals nearly $3,000,000.

15. If in 1985 IPSA had raised the registration fee by $100, and assuming that the elasticities of demand are such that this step reduced registration from 1,763 to 1,500, then the amount raised would have been $150,000—the sum

provided by the French government. The point is not to suggest that IPSA erred in accepting the French invitation. It is rather that IPSA cannot always expect such bounty and must be able to select congress sites to meet its own needs irrespective of the host government's ability to finance some of the institutional costs.

16. The cost need not be too great in financial terms if various national associations are willing to participate; more difficult will be the task of persuading some scholars in research-rich as well as research-poor countries that they should want to become involved in a true interchange of ideas with those who do not share their research paradigms, methodologies, and particular concerns.

APPENDIX A
Breakdown of Registrants by Country

	Official Tally	Questionnaires Sent	Questionnaires Returned	% Quest. Returned
North America				
United States	229	249	180	72
Canada	51	56	37	66
Total North American	280	305	217	71
Other Western (incl. Israel, Australia, and New Zealand)				
Germany (FRG)	64	67	26	39
France	42	41	8	20
Sweden	37	52	21	40
Spain	34	41	6	15
United Kingdom	34	42	20	48
Netherlands	32	31	18	58
Israel	29	31	7	23
Norway	21	23	13	57
Finland	20	27	10	37
Belgium	15	16	2	13
Denmark	12	14	10	71
Italy	12	16	3	19
Switzerland	11	13	6	46
Australia	6	8	3	38
Greece	4	5	3	60
Ireland	3	1	1	100
New Zealand	3	1	0	0
Luxembourg	2	2	0	0
Austria	1	1	0	0
Total Other Western	382	432	157	36
Third World: Latin America				
Mexico	47	123	8	7
Brazil	11	11	3	27
Venezuela	5	8	0	0
Argentina	3	6	0	0
Chile	1	1	1	100
	(67)	(149)	(12)	(8)

	Official Tally	Questionnaires Sent	Questionnaires Returned	% Quest. Returned
Third World: Africa and Middle East				
Turkey	22	19	7	37
Nigeria	4	10	1	10
Algeria	2	0	-	-
Cameroun	1	2	0	0
Ivory Coast	1	1	1	100
Jordan	1	1	0	0
Sierra Leone	1	1	0	0
Zambia	0	1	0	0
	(32)	(35)	(9)	(26)
Third World: Asia and Pacific				
India	32	33	7	21
Japan	30	39	10	26
Korea (South)	21	23	4	17
Thailand	2	2	0	0
China	0	1	0	0
Hong Kong	1	1	1	100
Indonesia	1	1	0	0
Malaysia	1	1	1	100
Pakistan	1	1	0	0
Philippines	1	2	1	50
Singapore	1	1	1	100
Taiwan	0	1	0	100
	(91)	(106)	(25)	(24)
Total Third World	190	290	46	16
Total	852	1027	420	41

APPENDIX B
Questionnaires

Quest. # _____

1-2 | 2 1
3-5

IntSci
7/80

1. Questionnaire for Registrants

University of Illinois

Department of Political Science

All information that would permit identification of the individual will be held in strict confidence, will be used only by persons engaged in and for the purposes of the survey, and will not be disclosed or released to others for any purpose.

(Please circle one answer code number unless otherwise instructed.)

1. How frequently do you attend the annual (or other regular) meetings of your national political science association (e.g. Indian Political Science Association, Deutsche Vereinigung für Politische Wissenschaft, American Political Science Association)?

    Almost every year 1   6

    Approximately every other year 2

    Less often than that 3

    Never 4

    No national political science association . 5

    National association does not hold meetings 6

2. What value does attending the annual meetings of your national political science association have

    a. For you personally? _____   7-8

    _____

    b. For most attendants (in your view)? _____   9-10

    _____

3a. Are you able to communicate effectively in one or more foreign languages (that is, a language other than that of the country in which you are now working) with scholars from other countries on matters of mutual scientific interest?

    Yes 1   11

    No *(Skip to Q.4a)* 2

    b. In what foreign language(s)? _____   12
    _____   13-19

4a. In what languages do you read journals, books, or other research reports in obtaining scientific information relevant to your research and/or teaching?

    (1) Native language(s) *(Specify which)* _____   20
        21-27

    (2) Language(s) currently used in teaching, if different from native language(s) *(Specify which)*   28
    _____   29-35

    (3) Other languages read *(Specify which)* _____   36
    _____   37-43

APPENDICES 147

4b. During 1979, did you read any scientific works in these foreign languages?

          Yes 1   44

          No *(Skip to Q.5a)* 2

 c. For each scientific work read in a foreign language, please indicate (a) the language and (b) the type of work (such as journal article, book, manuscript):

  (a) Language   (b) Type of Written Work

  _____   _____   45-52

  _____   _____

  _____   _____

  _____   _____

5a. Have you ever attended any international scientific meetings or international conferences <u>within</u> the country in which you are now working?

          Yes 1   53

          No *(Skip to Q.6a)* 2

 b. How many such international conferences have you ever attended? *(Please give approximate number)*

                 _____   54

6a. Have you ever been outside the country in which you are now working on a trip for scholarly purposes which lasted more than three months?

          Yes 1   55

          No *(Skip to Q.7a)* 2

 b. How many times have you made such a trip? *(Please give approximate number)*

                 _____   56

7a. How many international scientific meetings or international scholarly conferences <u>outside</u> the country in which you are now working have you attended? *(Please give approximate number--if none indicate 0)*

                 _____   57

 b. What group(s) sponsored these meetings or conferences? _____   58-67

_____

_____

_____

8. It is sometimes said that international scientific congresses in the field of political science serve a variety of functions--for the individual participant, the political science profession as a whole, and the host country.
   a. What do you consider to be the chief functions of such international conferences for the <u>individual participant</u>?

   _____ 68-69

   _____

   b. What do you consider to be the chief functions of such international conferences for the <u>political science profession as a whole</u>?

   _____ 70-71

   _____

   c. What do you consider to be the chief functions of such international conferences for the <u>host country</u>?

   _____ 72-73

   _____

9. From your own perspective, how important are these functions . . .

	Very important	Somewhat important	Not very important	Not at all important	
a. For the individual participant? . . .	1	2	3	4	74
b. For political science profession? . .	1	2	3	4	75
c. For the host country?	1	2	3	4	76

10. Taking everything into consideration, what do you think is the single chief value of international scientific congresses in the field of political science?

    _____ 77-78

    _____

11. Did you attend the World Congress of the International Political Science Association held in

		Yes	No	
a.	Geneva, Switzerland in 1964?	1	2	79
b.	Brussels, Belgium in 1967?	1	2	80 1-2 | 2 2 3-5 | DUP
c.	Munich, West Germany in 1970?	1	2	6
d.	Montreal, Canada in 1973?	1	2	7
e.	Edinburgh, Scotland in 1976?	1	2	8

APPENDICES 149

12a. Did you attend the 1979 World Congress of the International Political Science Association, held in Moscow, Soviet Union?

             Yes 1   9

             No 2

 b. Why did you decide (to attend/not to attend) the 1979 IPSA World Congress in Moscow? *(Please list all relevant reasons)*

  _____ 10-19

  _____

 c. If you gave more than one reason, which of these was the <u>single</u> most decisive reason for your decision?

  _____ 20-21

  _____

13a. In 1976 the Council and Executive Committee of the International Political Science Association decided to accept the Soviet Union's invitation to hold the 1979 IPSA World Congress in Moscow. Given the international circumstances of the mid-1970s, do you think that this decision was a good one?

             Yes 1   22

             No 2

 b. Please explain your response in a brief sentence or two.

  _____ 23-24

  _____

14a. More generally, is it a good idea to hold scientific meetings in the Soviet Union?

             Yes 1   25

             No 2

 b. Please explain your response in a brief sentence or two.

  _____ 26-27

  _____

(IF YOU DID <u>NOT</u> ATTEND THE 1979 IPSA WORLD CONGRESS IN MOSCOW, PLEASE SKIP TO Q.29a, PAGE 12)

15. Had you ever been to the Soviet Union before attending the IPSA World Congress in Moscow in August 1979?

             Yes 1   28

             No 2

16. We would like to know about some of your expectations with respect to the IPSA World Congress in Moscow and the extent to which your experience matched these expectations. For each of the following statements you are provided with a set of possible responses indicating how closely the statement describes your expectations, and another set indicating how closely the statement in fact describes what you experienced in the Soviet Union. Space is also provided for you to elaborate upon your feelings, should you wish to do so.

	Expectation				Experience			
	Not at all what I expected	Only a little like I expected	Approximately what I expected	Exactly what I expected	Not at all what actually happened	Only a little like what happened	Approximately what happened	Exactly what happened
a. The accommodations (including hotel and provision for meals) would be adequate to my needs	1	2	3	4 29	1	2	3	4 30
Comment:								
b. I would have little social contact with people in the USSR (other than Congress participants) .	1	2	3	4 31	1	2	3	4 32
Comment:								
c. I would have a great deal of contact with Soviet scholars at the Congress	1	2	3	4 33	1	2	3	4 34
Comment:								
d. I would have a great deal of contact with other East European scholars at the Congress	1	2	3	4 35	1	2	3	4 36
Comment:								

APPENDICES   151

	Expectation				Experience			
	Not at all what I expected	Only a little like I expected	Approximately what I expected	Exactly what I expected	Not at all what actually happened	Only a little like what happened	Approximately what happened	Exactly what happened
e. The organization of the Congress itself would facilitate interaction among participants	1	2	3	4 37	1	2	3	4 38
Comment: _____								
f. A substantial number of Congress participants would have research interests similar to my own	1	2	3	4 39	1	2	3	4 40
Comment: _____								
g. I would learn something professionally useful from papers and comments presented in the formal sessions by Soviet and East European participants	1	2	3	4 41	1	2	3	4 42
Comment: _____								
h. Participants in formal sessions would be able to raise any topics and present any points of view they wished (even on highly contentious "cold war" issues)	1	2	3	4 43	1	2	3	4 44
Comment: _____								

152 SCIENCE, POLITICS, AND INTERNATIONAL CONFERENCES

	Expectation				Experience			
	Not at all what I expected	Only a little like I expected	Approximately what I expected	Exactly what I expected	Not at all what actually happened	Only a little like what happened	Approximately what happened	Exactly what happened
i. The procedures followed by panel chairpersons would encourage uninhibited discussion and the presentation of a wide range of viewpoints . . . Comment:	1	2	3	4 45	1	2	3	4 46
j. There would be opportunities for informal interaction with Congress participants from other countries that would contribute to my ongoing and future research . . . Comment:	1	2	3	4 47	1	2	3	4 48
k. Overall, my visit to the IPSA World Congress in Moscow would be a satisfying personal experience . . . Comment:	1	2	3	4 49	1	2	3	4 50

17. About how much informal contact would you say you had with the following kinds of people during your visit to the 1979 IPSA World Congress?

		No contact at all	Very little contact	Occasional contact	Great deal of contact	
a.	Colleagues from your own country	1	2	3	4	51
b.	Soviet scholars	1	2	3	4	52
c.	Other East European scholars	1	2	3	4	53

Colleagues from countries other than your own in:

d.	West Europe and North America	1	2	3	4	54
e.	Third World	1	2	3	4	55

18a. Considering the Congress as a whole and all interactions with Congress participants, did you receive information that led to a major modification in any of your work activities?

    Yes 1   56
    No *(Skip to Q.19)* 2

b. How did you receive this information?

    Oral presentation of paper . 1   57
    Reading copy of paper 2
    Floor discussion 3
    Informal contacts 4
    Other *(Specify)* _____ 5

c. What type of activity was modified by this interaction?

    Research 1   58
    Teaching 2
    Manuscript/publication plans 3
    Applied work 4
    Administration 5
    Other *(Specify)* _____ 6

d. Please describe the nature of this modification.

_____   59-60
_____
_____

19. Since the IPSA World Congress in Moscow, in which of the following ways have you kept up contacts with colleagues you met for the first time from . . .
(Circle all answer code numbers that apply)

		a. USSR & Eastern Europe?	b. Western Europe?	c. Third World?	d. North America?
(1)	I have not tried to keep up contacts	1	1	1	1 61-64
(2)	Through correspondence	2	2	2	2 65-68
(3)	Scientific meetings and conferences	3	3	3	3 69-72
(4)	Visits or exchange of visits	4	4	4	4 73-76
(5)	Exchange of reprints, papers	5	5	5	5 77-80 / 1-2 23 / 3-5 DUP
(6)	Joint or parallel research	6	6	6	6 5-9
(7)	Joint publication	7	7	7	7 10-13
(8)	My attempts to maintain contacts have been unsuccessful	8	8	8	8 14-17
(9)	Other *(Specify)* _____	9	9	9	9 18-21

20a. What was the **best** panel you attended at the Moscow Congress?

_____   22-24

b. Why was this the best? _____   25-26

_____

21a. What was the **worst** panel you attended at the Moscow Congress?

_____   27-29

b. Why was this the worst? _____   30-31

_____

22a. Did you encounter any scientific communication problems which you believe should be corrected before the next IPSA World Congress?

          Yes 1 32

          No *(Skip to Q.23a)* 2

b. What changes do you think might help prevent such scientific communication problems at future IPSA world congresses?

_____   33-34

_____

23a. Did you participate in one of the pre-Congress or post-Congress tours organized for IPSA participants?

                              Yes 1   35

                              No *(Skip to Q.24)* 2

   b. What was the major destination of the tour?

                              Leningrad-Kiev-Vladimir . . . 1   36

                              Baltic 2

                              Caucausus 3

                              Soviet Asia 4

                              Other *(Specify)* _____ 5

   c. How would you evaluate this tour? Would you say it was . . .

                              Very worthwhile 1   37

                              Somewhat worthwhile 2

                              Not very worthwhile 3

                              Not at all worthwhile 4

24. Overall, how would you rate your experience at the IPSA World Congress in Moscow? Were you . . .

                              Very satisfied 1   38

                              Somewhat satisfied 2

                              Not very satisfied 3

                              Not at all satisfied 4

25a. If you have attended more than one IPSA World Congress, which <u>single</u> one do consider to have been the most worthwhile, overall?

                    IPSA Congress earlier than 1964 1   39

                  1964: Geneva, Switzerland 2

                  1967: Brussels, Belgium 3

                  1970: Munich, West Germany 4

                  1973: Montreal, Canada 5

                  1976: Edinburgh, Scotland 6

                  1979: Moscow, Soviet Union 7

                  Have only attended one IPSA world congress . 8

25b. Why? _____ 40-41

_____

26a. Some critics of the IPSA World Congress in Moscow complained that the Soviet government used the meeting for its own propagandistic purposes. Do you . . .

         Strongly agree? 1   42

         Agree somewhat? 2

         Disagree somewhat? 3

         Strongly disagree? 4

 b. Why are you of this opinion? _____ 43-44

_____

27a. Most of us, before we went to the IPSA World Congress in Moscow, had an *image* of the Soviet Union, that is, some "picture in our mind" of what we believed to be true (irrespective of whether or not we liked the image we saw). How did your experience during the course of your visit affect your *image* of the Soviet Union?

      Reinforced existing image *(Skip to Q.28a)* 1   45

      Did not change image *(Skip to Q.28a)*. 2

      Significantly changed image 3

 b. In what way did your experience change your image of the Soviet Union?

_____ 46-47

28a. Did attending the IPSA World Congress change your *attitude* toward (a) the Soviet government or (b) the people of the Soviet Union?

               Government People

        Yes 1   48   1   49

        No 2   2

 b. How did it change your attitude?

      Very much in positive direction 1   50   1   51

      Somewhat in positive direction 2   2

      Somewhat in negative direction 3   3

      Very much in negative direction 4   4

      Did not change my attitude 5   5

28c. Please elaborate on how your attitude changed toward the . . .

Soviet government _____ 52-53

_____

People of the Soviet Union _____ 54-55

_____

29a. As you may have heard, the next World Congress of the International Political Science Association will be held in August 1982 in Rio de Janeiro, Brazil. Are you thinking of attending this meeting?

                        Yes 1   56

                        No *(Skip to Q.30a)* 2

   b. On what circumstances does your decision to attend the 1982 IPSA World Congress depend?

_____ 57-58

_____

30a. Do you think that Rio de Janeiro is an appropriate site for an IPSA World Congress?

                        Yes 1   59

                        No 2

   b. Please explain your response in a brief sentence or two.

_____ 60-61

_____

31. What three themes would you most like to see included in the official program for the 1982 IPSA World Congress in Rio de Janeiro?

   a. _____ 62-63

   b. _____ 64-65

   c. _____ 66-67

32a. It has been proposed that the 1985 IPSA World Congress be held in Paris, France. Do you think that Paris is an appropriate site for this meeting?

           Yes 1   68

           No *(Skip to Q.33)* 2

 b. Please explain your response in a brief sentence or two.

  _____   69-70

  _____

33. In what city would you like to see future IPSA World Congresses held? *(Please list three cities rank-ordered in terms of your own preference.)*

 a. _____   71-72

 b. _____   73-74

 c. _____   75-76

34a. With what type of institution are your currently affiliated?

     Academic 1   77

     Government 2

     Industry 3

     Private research organization 4

     Governmental research organization 5

     Other *(Specify)* _____ 6

 b. In what country is this located? _____   78-79 / 1-2 | 24 / 3-5 | DUP

 c. What is your title? _____   6-7

 d. In what year did you begin your professional career as a political scientist?

                     _____   8-9

35. Within the discipline of political science, what is the <u>primary</u> focus of your teaching and/or research? *(Circle one only)*

        Political institutions and processes of your own country . . 1   10

        Public law (including jurisprudence) 2

        Public policy and administration 3

        Political behavior 4

        Normative or empirical theory, philosophy 5

        Comparative politics 6

        International relations 7

        Methodology 8

        Other *(Specify)* _____ 9

36a. Do your teaching/research interests have a geographic focus?

        Yes 1   11

        No *(Skip to Q.37a)*. 2

  b. Is this geographic focus regional or global?

        Regional 1   12

        Global *(Skip to Q.37a)*. . . . 2

  c. What is the specific region? _____   13-14

37a. What is the most advanced degree you have earned? _____   15-16

  b. At what institution was this degree awarded? _____   17-18

38. In what year were you born? _____   19-20

39. What is your sex?

        Female 1   21

        Male 2

40. Which one of the following best describes your interests?

    My interests are very heavily in research 1   22

    My interests are very heavily in teaching 2

    My interests are in both, but lean more toward research 3

    My interests are in both, but lean more toward teaching 4

    My interests are in neither research nor teaching but rather in *(Please specify)* _____ 5

41. How many books or monographs have you published or edited, alone or in collaboration?

    None 1   23
    1-2 2
    3-4 3
    5-10 4
    More than 10 . . . 5

42. How many articles have you published in academic or professional journals?

    None 1   24
    1-2 2
    3-4 3
    5-10 4
    11-20 5
    21-30 6
    31-50 7
    More than 50 . . . 8

43. How many of your professional writings have been published or accepted for publication in the last two years?

    One 1   25
    Two 2
    Three 3
    Four 4
    Five 5
    Six-ten 6
    More than ten . . . 7
    None 8

THANK YOU VERY MUCH.

APPENDICES 161

PolSci
7/80

Quest. # _____

2. Questionnaire for Nonregistrants

University of Illinois
Department of Political Science

All information that would permit identification of the individual will be held in strict confidence, will be used only by persons engaged in and for the purposes of the survey, and will not be disclosed or released to others for any purpose.

(Please circle one answer code number unless otherwise instructed.)

1. How frequently do you attend the annual meetings of . . .

	Almost every year	Approximately every other year	Less often than that	Never
a. Your national political science association (e.g. American or Canadian Political Science Association)?	1	2	3	4
b. Your regional political science association (e.g. Midwest Political Science Association)?	1	2	3	4
c. A subdisciplinary association (e.g. International Studies Association)?	1	2	3	4

2. What value does attending each of the following have for (a) you personally and (b) most attendants?

	a. Personal value	b. Value for attendants
(1) Your national political science association?		
(2) Your regional political science association?		
(3) A subdisciplinary association?		

3a. Are you able to communicate effectively in one or more foreign languages (that is, a language other than that of the country in which you are now working) with scholars from other countries on matters of mutual scientific interest?

                              Yes 1   21

                              No *(Skip to Q.4a)* 2

   b. In what foreign language(s)? _____   22-29

4a. Have you ever attended any international scientific meetings or international conferences <u>within</u> the country in which you are now working?

                              Yes 1   30

                              No *(Skip to Q.5a)* 2

   b. How many such international conferences have you ever attended?
      (Please give approximate number) _____   31

5a. Have you ever been outside the country in which you are now working on a trip for scholarly purposes which lasted more than three months?

                              Yes 1   32

                              No *(Skip to Q.6a)* 2

   b. How many times have you made such a trip?
      (Please give approximate number) _____   33

6a. Have you ever attended any international scientific meetings or international conferences <u>outside</u> the country in which you are now working?

                              Yes 1   34

                              No *(Skip to Q.7a)* 2

   b. How many such international conferences have you ever attended?
      (Please give approximate number) _____   35

8. It is sometimes said that international scientific congresses in the field of political science serve a variety of functions--for the individual participant, the political science profession as a whole, and the host country.

   a. What do you consider to be the chief functions of such international conferences for the <u>individual participant</u>?

_____   36-37

_____

_____

8b. What do you consider to be the chief functions of such international conferences for the <u>political science profession as a whole</u>?

_____ 38-39

_____

c. What do you consider to be the chief functions of such international conferences for the <u>host country</u>?

_____ 40-41

_____

9. From your own perspective, how important are these functions . . .

	Very important	Somewhat important	Not very important	Not at all important	
a. For the individual participant?	1	2	3	4	42
b. For political science profession? . . .	1	2	3	4	43
c. For the host country?	1	2	3	4	44

10. Taking everything into consideration, what do you think is the single chief value of international scientific congresses in the field of political science?

_____ 45-46

_____

11. Did you attend the World Congresses of the International Political Science Association held in . . .

	Yes	No	
a. Geneva, Switzerland in 1964?	1	2	47
b. Brussels, Belgium in 1967?	1	2	48
c. Munich, West Germany in 1970?	1	2	49
d. Montreal, Canada in 1973?	1	2	50
e. Edinburgh, Scotland in 1976?	1	2	51

12a. Did you attend the 1979 World Congress of the International Political Science Association, held in Moscow, Soviet Union?

　　　　　　　　　　　　　　Yes 1   52
　　　　　　　　　　　　　　No 2

12b. Why did you decide (to attend/not to attend) the 1979 IPSA World Congress in Moscow? *(Please list all relevant reasons)*

_____ 53-62

_____

_____

c. If you gave more than one reason, which of these was the <u>single</u> most decisive reason for your decision?

_____ 63-64

13a. In 1976 the Council and Executive Committee of the International Political Science Association decided to accept the Soviet Union's invitation to hold the 1979 IPSA World Congress in Moscow. Given the international circumstances of the mid-1970s, do you think that this decision was a good one?

                                        Yes 1   65

                                        No 2

b. Please explain your response in a brief sentence or two.

_____ 66-67

_____

_____

14a. More generally, is it a good idea to hold scientific meetings in the Soviet Union?

                                        Yes 1   68

                                        No 2

b. Please explain your response in a brief sentence or two.

_____ 69-70

_____

_____

15a. As you may have heard, the next World Gongress of the International Political Science Association will be held in August 1982 in Rio de Janeiro, Brazil. Are you thinking of attending this meeting?

                                        Yes 1   71

                                        No *(Skip to Q.16a)* 2

15b. On what circumstances does your decision to attend the 1982 IPSA World Congress depend?

_____
_____

16a. Do you think that Rio de Janeiro is an appropriate site for an IPSA World Congress?

                                   Yes 1

                                   No 2

b. Please explain your response in a brief sentence or two.

_____
_____
_____

17. What three themes would you most like to see included in the official program for the 1982 IPSA World Congress in Rio de Janeiro?

    a. _____

    b. _____

    c. _____

18a. It has been proposed that the 1985 IPSA World Congress be held in Paris, France. Do you think that Paris is an appropriate site for this meeting?

                                   Yes 1

                                   No 2

b. Please explain your response in a brief sentence or two.

_____
_____
_____

19. In what city would you like to see future IPSA World Congresses held? *(Please list three cities rank-ordered in terms of your own preference.)*

    a. _____ 11-12

    b. _____ 13-14

    c. _____ 15-16

20a. With what type of institution are you currently affiliated?

    Academic 1   17

    Government 2

    Industry 3

    Private research organization 4

    Governmental research organization 5

    Other *(Specify)* _____ 6

  b. In what country is this located? _____ 18-19

  c. What is your title? _____ 20-21

  d. In what year did you begin your professional career as a political scientist?

                                                                                             _____ 22-23

21. Within the discipline of political science, what is the **primary** focus of your teaching and/or research? *(Circle one only)*

    Political institutions and processes of your own country . . 1   24

    Public law (including jurisprudence) 2

    Public policy and administration 3

    Political behavior 4

    Normative or empirical theory, philosophy 5

    Comparative politics 6

    International relations 7

    Methodology 8

    Other *(Specify)* _____ 9

22a. Do your teaching/research interests have a geographic focus?

                             Yes 1   25

                             No *(Skip to Q.23a)*. 2

22b. Is this geographic focus regional or global?

>>> Regional 1   26
>>> Global *(Skip to Q.23a)* . . . 2

c. What is the specific region? _____   27-28

23a. What is the most advanced degree you have earned? _____   29-30

b. At what institution was this degree awarded? _____   31-32

24. In what year were you born? _____   33-34

25. What is your sex?
>>> Female 1   35
>>> Male 2

26. Which one of the following best describes your interests?

>> My interests are very heavily in research 1   36
>> My interests are very heavily in teaching 2
>> My interests are in both, but lean more toward research 3
>> My interests are in both, but lean more toward teaching 4
>> My interests are in neither research nor teaching but rather in
>> *(Please specify)* _____ 5

27. How many books or monographs have you published or edited, alone or in collaboration?

>>> None 1   37
>>> 1-2 2
>>> 3-4 3
>>> 5-10 4
>>> More than 10 . . . 5

28. How many articles have you published in academic or professional journals?

    None 1   38
    1-2 2
    3-4 3
    5-10 4
    11-20 5
    21-30 6
    31-50 7
    More than 50 . . . 8

29. How many of your professional writings have been published or accepted for publication <u>in the last two years</u>?

    One 1   39
    Two 2
    Three 3
    Four 4
    Five 5
    Six-ten 6
    More than ten . . . 7
    None 8

THANK YOU VERY MUCH.

APPENDIX C
Scales of Professionalism and Internationalism

C.1. Professional Activity Scale

Score	Registrants North American	Registrants Other Western	Registrants Third World	Registrants Total	Non-registrants
0	1%	1%	0%	1%	10%
1	1	1	7	1	11
2	7	3	4	5	15
3	7	4	4	6	12
4	11	15	9	12	18
5	16	22	24	19	12
6	18	16	11	16	12
7	20	13	11	17	6
8	11	13	17	12	3
9	8	8	9	8	2
10	2	5	4	3	0
Total*	100%	100%	100%	100%	100%
Mean	5.8	6.0	5.8	5.9	3.6
Std. mean**	5.8	6.0	5.8	5.9	3.6

*Columns may not add up to 100 percent because of rounding.
**Mean scores standardized to a scale ranging from 0 to 10.

Scoring:
Attendance at national political science association meetings (2 = almost every year; 1 = every other year; 0 = less often or never)
Research vs. teaching interest (2 = heavily research; 1 = leaning toward research; 0 = other)
Published books and monographs (2 = 5 or more; 1 = between 1 and 4; 0 = none)
Published articles (2 = 21 or more; 1 = between 3 and 20; 0 = 2 or fewer)
Publications in last 2 years (2 = 6 or more; 1 = between 2 and 5; 0 = 1 or none)

C.2. Professional Status Scale

	Registrants				Non-registrants
Score	North American	Other Western	Third World	Total	
0	2%	3%	4%	2%	6%
1	2	6	2	3	12
2	6	8	9	7	16
3	12	17	13	14	19
4	18	14	22	17	18
5	19	17	13	18	12
6	17	14	9	15	8
7	15	17	15	15	8
8	10	5	11	8	1
Total*	100%	100%	100%	100%	100%
Mean	5.0	4.6	4.7	4.8	3.5
Std. mean**	6.3	5.7	5.8	6.0	4.3

*Columns may not add up to 100 percent because of rounding.
**Mean scores standardized to a scale ranging from 0 to 10.

Scoring:
Level of highest degree (1 = Ph.D. or equivalent; 0 = other)
Title (1 = professor, president, dean, director, senior researcher, or equivalent; 0 = assistant or associate professor, graduate assistant, researcher, or equivalent)
Seniority, as indicated by year entered professional career (2 = 1922–1959; 1 = 1960–1972; 0 = 1973 or later)
Published books and monographs (2 = 5 or more; 1 = between 1 and 4; 0 = none)
Published articles (2 = 21 or more; 1 = between 3 and 20; 0 = 2 or fewer)

C.3. International Research Competence Scale

	Registrants				Non-registrants
Score	North American	Other Western	Third World	Total	
0	10%	3%	0%	6%	45%
1	15	4	9	10	22
2	24	13	22	20	16
3	17	31	37	25	11
4	21	28	20	23	5
5	13	21	13	16	0
Total*	100%	100%	100%	100%	100%
Mean	2.6	3.4	3.1	3.0	1.1
Std. mean**	5.3	6.8	6.1	5.9	2.2

*Columns may not add up to 100 percent because of rounding.
**Mean scores standardized to a scale ranging from 0 to 10.

Scoring:
Number of foreign languages usable for scientific communication (2 = two or more; 1 = one; 0 = none)
Actual use of foreign languages for research (1 = yes; 0 = no)
Number of research trips overseas (2 = three or more; 1 = one or two; 3 = none)

C.4. International Activity Scale

Score	Registrants				Non-registrants
	North American	Other Western	Third World	Total	
0	0%	1%	0%	0%	18%
1	4	3	4	4	24
2	9	4	17	8	18
3	20	14	7	16	14
4	18	17	26	19	8
5	15	21	17	17	8
6	18	19	9	17	4
7	8	12	2	9	5
8	7	8	9	7	1
9	2	1	9	3	0
Total*	100%	100%	100%	100%	100%
Mean	4.6	5.0	4.7	4.8	2.4
Std. mean**	5.2	5.6	5.2	5.3	2.7

*Columns may not add up to 100 percent because of rounding.
**Mean scores standardized to a scale ranging from 0 to 10.

Scoring:
Number of times attended ISCs in own country (2 = six or more; 1 = between one and five; 0 = none)
Number of research trips overseas (2 = three or more; 1 = one or two; 3 = none)
Number of times attended ISCs overseas (2 = six or more; 1 = between one and five; 0 = none)
Field of specialization (1 = comparative or international politics; 0 = other)
Geographic focus of teaching and research (2 = global; 1 = regional; 0 = national or other)

C.5. IPSA Experience Scale

Score	Registrants				Non-registrants
	North American	Other Western	Third World	Total	
0	54%	47%	74%	53%	90%
1	18	24	15	20	6
2	17	12	11	14	3
3	6	10	0	7	1
4	4	5	0	4	0
5	2	3	0	2	0
Total*	100%	100%	100%	100%	100%
Mean	0.9	1.1	0.4	1.0	0.2
Std. mean**	1.9	2.2	0.7	1.9	0.3

*Columns may not add up to 100 percent because of rounding.
**Mean scores standardized to a scale ranging from 0 to 10.

Scoring:
Attended Geneva world congress, 1964 (1 = yes; 0 = no)
Attended Brussels world congress, 1967 (1 = yes; 0 = no)
Attended Munich world congress, 1970 (1 = yes; 0 = no)
Attended Montréal world congress, 1973 (1 = yes; 0 = no)
Attended Edinburgh world congress, 1976 (1 = yes; 0 = no)

Bibliography

ALGER, Chadwick F. and Gene M. LYONS (1974) "Social science as a transnational system: report of a seminar." *International Studies Notes*, 1,3 (Fall): 1-13.
ALKER, Hayward R., Jr. (1978) "The politics of peace." *Participation*, 2,3: 23-31.
ANGELL, Robert Cooley (1981) "Do ISPAs promote global integration?" pp. 237-254 in William M. Evan (ed.), *Knowledge and Power in a Global Society*. Beverly Hills, Calif.: Sage Publications.
———. (1969) *Peace on the March: Transnational Participation*. New York: Van Nostrand Reinhold.
ATELSEK, Frank J. and Irene L. GOMBERG (1981) *An Analysis of Travel by Academic Scientists and Engineers to International Scientific Meetings in 1979-80*. Washington, D.C.: American Council on Education.
BARBER, Bernard (1968) "The sociology of science," pp. 92-100 in David L. Sills (ed.), *International Encyclopedia of the Social Sciences*, vol. 14. New York: Crowell Collier and Macmillan.
BARENTS, J. (1959) "Vanity fair? or, international congresses reconsidered." *American Political Science Review*, 53,4 (December): 1090-1094.
BECKER, Howard S. and Irving Louis HOROWITZ (1972) "Radical politics and sociological research." *American Journal of Sociology*, 78,1 (July): 48-66.
BOSE, Nirmal (1978) "The politics of development and system change." *Participation*, 2,3: 43-55.
BROADHEAD, Robert C. and Ray C. RIST (1976) "Gatekeepers and the social control of social research." *Social Problems*, 23,3 (February): 325-326.
BROWN, Archie (1984) "Political science in the Soviet Union: a new stage of development?" *Soviet Studies*, 36,3 (July): 317-344.
CANCIAN, Francesca M. (1968) "Varieties of functional analysis," pp. 29-43 in David L. Sills (ed.), *International Encyclopedia of the Social Sciences*, vol. 6. New York: Crowell Collier and Macmillan.
CAPES, Mary [ed.] (1960) *Communication or Conflict: Conferences: Their*

Nature, Dynamics, and Planning. New York: Association Press.
COLLINS, H. M. (1983a) "An empirical relativist programme in the sociology of scientific knowledge," pp. 85-113 in Karin D. Knorr-Cetina and Michael Mulkay (eds.), *Science Observed: Perspectives on the Social Study of Science.* London and Beverly Hills, Calif.: Sage Publications.
——— . (1983b) "The sociology of scientific knowledge: studies of contemporary science." *Annual Review of Sociology,* 9: 265-285.
CRANE, Diana (1981) "Alternative models of ISPAs," pp. 29-47 in William M. Evan (ed.), *Knowledge and Power in a Global Society.* Beverly Hills, Calif.: Sage Publications.
——— . (1972) *Invisible Colleges: Diffusion of Knowledge in Scientific Communities.* Chicago and London: The University of Chicago Press.
——— . (1971) "Transnational networks in basic science." *International Organization,* 25,3 (Summer): 585-601.
——— . (1970) "The nature of scientific communication and influence." *International Social Science Journal,* 22,1: 28-41.
DICKSON, David (1979) "Brazil bans conference on Amazon biology." *Nature,* 277,2 (February): 340.
EVAN, William M. [ed.] (1981a) *Knowledge and Power in a Global Society.* Beverly Hills, Calif.: Sage Publications.
——— . (1981b) "Some dilemmas of knowledge and power: an introduction," pp. 11-25 in William M. Evan (ed.), *Knowledge and Power in a Global Society.* Beverly Hills, Calif.: Sage Publications.
——— . (1975) "The International Sociological Association and the internationalization of sociology." *International Social Science Journal,* 27,2: 385-393.
FIGHIERA, Gian Carlo (1984) "The geographical distribution of meetings throughout the world." *International Transnational Associations,* 36,3 (July-August): 142-159.
GINIGER, Henry (1979) "Canadian ousted by Soviet hints 'gulag justice' is not monolithic." *The New York Times* (3 September): A4.
HAGSTROM, Warren O. (1965) *The Scientific Community.* New York: Basic Books.
HANSON, Elizabeth C. and Richard L. MERRITT (1983) "International conferences as a mode of technology transfer." *World Policy,* no. 1: 1-8.
INTERNATIONAL COUNCIL OF SCIENTIFIC UNIONS (1976) *The Free Circulation of Scientists: Advice to Organizers of International Scientific Meetings.* Paris: ICSU Secretariat.
JAGTENBERG, Tom (1983) *The Social Construction of Science: A Comparative Study of Goal Direction, Research Evolution and Legitimation.* Dordrecht, Holland: D. Reidel.
JOHNS HOPKINS UNIVERSITY, Center for Research in Scientific Communication (1968) *Reports of the American Psychological Association's Project on Scientific Information Exchange in Psychology* (2 vols). Washington, D.C.: American Psychological Association.
KAPLAN, Norman and Norman W. STORER (1968) "Scientific communication," pp. 112-117 in David L. Sills (ed.), *International*

Encyclopedia of the Social Sciences, vol. 14. New York: Crowell Collier and Macmillan.
KELMAN, Herbert C. [ed.] (1965) *International Behavior: A Social-Psychological Approach*. New York: Holt, Rinehart and Winston.
KNORR-CETINA, Karin D. and Michael MULKAY (1983) "Introduction: emerging principles in social studies of science," pp. 1-17 in Karin D. Knorr-Cetina and Michael Mulkay (eds.), *Science Observed: Perspectives on the Social Study of Science*. London and Beverly Hills, Calif.: Sage Publications.
KOCHEN, Manfred (1985) "Social know-how and its role in invention and innovation," pp. 269-289 in Richard L. Merritt and Anna J. Merritt (eds.), *Innovation in the Public Sector*. Beverly Hills, Calif.: Sage Publications.
KRIESBERG, Louis (1981) "Varieties of ISPAs: their forms and functions," pp. 49-68 in William M. Evan (ed.), *Knowledge and Power in a Global Society*. Beverly Hills, Calif.: Sage Publications.
KUHN, Thomas (1970) *The Structure of Scientific Revolutions* (rev. enl. ed.). Chicago: University of Chicago Press.
LADD, Everett Carll, Jr. and Seymour Martin LIPSET (1978) "The Ladd-Lipset survey: faculty members who travel abroad." *The Chronicle of Higher Education*, 16,9 (24 April): 8.
LAKOFF, Sanford A. (1977) "Scientists, technologists and political power," pp. 355-391 in Ina Spiegel-Rösing and Derek de Solla Price (eds.), *Science, Technology and Society: A Cross-Disciplinary Perspective*. London and Beverly Hills, Calif.: Sage Publications.
LASSWELL, Harold D. and Abraham KAPLAN (1950) *Power and Society: A Framework for Political Inquiry*. New Haven: Yale University Press.
LEVY, Marion J., Jr. (1968) "Structural-functional analysis," pp. 21-29 in David L. Sills (ed.), *International Encyclopedia of the Social Sciences*, vol. 6. New York: Crowell Collier and Macmillan.
LODGE, David (1984) *Small World: An Academic Romance*. New York: Macmillan.
LUDZ, Peter C. (1979) "Cumulative growth in political knowledge since 1950." *Participation*, 3,1: 46-51.
MACIVER, Robert M. (1947) *The Web of Government*. New York: Macmillan.
MARCSON, Simon (1972) "Research settings," pp. 161-191 in Saad Z. Nagi and Ronald G. Corwin (eds.), *The Social Contexts of Research*. New York: John Wiley and Sons, Wiley-Interscience.
MEAD, Margaret (1968) "Conferences," pp. 215-220 in David L. Sills (ed.), *International Encyclopedia of the Social Sciences*, vol. 3. New York: Crowell Collier and Macmillan.
MENZEL, Herbert (1959) "Planned and unplanned scientific communication," pp. 189-212 of *Proceedings of the International Conference on Scientific Information*; reprinted as pp. 417-441 in Bernard Barber and Walter Hirsch (eds.), *The Sociology of Science*. New York: The Free Press, 1962.
MERLE, Marcel (1978) "The politics of peace." *Participation*, 2,3: 39-42.
MERRITT, Richard L. (1980) "Communication." *PS*, 13:3 (Summer): 390-392.
——— and William SMIRNOV [eds.] (1979-1981) *International Political*

Science Enters the 1980s: Abstracts of papers presented at the XIth World Congress of the International Political Science Association, Moscow, U.S.S.R., August 12-18, 1979 (2 vols.). Ottawa, Ont.: International Political Science Association.

MERTON, Robert K. (1957) *Social Theory and Social Structure* (rev. enl. ed.). New York: The Free Press.

———. (1942) "A note on science and technology in a democratic order." *Journal of Legal and Political Sociology*, 1,1-2 (October): 115-126; reprinted as "Science and democratic social structure," pp. 550-561 in Merton (1957).

MEYNAUD, Jean (1961) "International co-operation in the field of the social sciences: a tentative balance-sheet," pp. 7-14 in UNESCO (ed.), *International Organizations in the Social Sciences*. Paris: UNESCO, Reports and Papers in the Social Sciences, no. 13; reprinted as pp. 103-115 in Philippart (1970).

——— and P. A. REYNOLDS (1956) "Third congress of the International Political Science Association: Stockholm, 21-27 August 1955." *International Social Science Bulletin*, 8,1: 191-197.

MILLER, James G. (1978) *Living Systems*. New York: McGraw-Hill.

MULKAY, Michael J. (1979) *Science and the Sociology of Knowledge*. London: George Allen and Unwin.

———. (1977) "Sociology of the scientific research community," pp. 93-148 in Ina Spiegel-Rösing and Derek de Solla Price (eds.), *Science, Technology and Society: A Cross-Disciplinary Perspective*. London and Beverly Hills, Calif.: Sage Publications.

NATIONAL SCIENCE BOARD (1981) *Science Indicators 1980*. Washington, D.C.: National Science Foundation.

NUTTIN, Joseph R. (1974) "Scientific communication and information exchange in an international congress setting." *International Associations*, 26:5 (May), 296-299, 273.

PEAR, Robert (1980) "U.S. bars exclusions of homosexual aliens in most circumstances." *The New York Times* (10 September): 20.

PHILIPPART, André [ed.] (1970) *Synthesis Report on the I.P.S.A.: 20 Years Activities, 1949-1969*. Paris: International Political Science Association.

POLANYI, Michael (1951) *The Logic of Liberty*. London: Routledge and Kegan Paul.

PRICE, Derek J. de Solla (1967) "Nations can public or perish." *Science & Technology*, no. 70 (October): 84-90.

———. (1961) *Science Since Babylon*. New Haven and London: Yale University Press.

ROOSEVELT, Curtis (1970) "The politics of development: a role for interest and pressure groups." *International Associations*, 22,5 (May): 283-289.

SCOHY, Michele. (1977) "Supplement of 1970-1976 to the synthesis report on the activities of the International Political Science Association." Ottawa: International Political Science Association.

SCULLY, Malcolm G. (1979) "Canada lifts ban on Marxist scholar." *The Chronicle of Higher Education*, 18:21 (30 July): 5.

SELTZER, Richard J. (1978) "Science, world politics, and human rights." *Chemical and Engineering News*, 56,8 (20 February): 34-47.
SEMENOV, Vadim S. (1978) "Cumulative growth in political knowledge since 1949." *Participation*, 2,3: 56-60.
SHAKHNAZAROV, Georgii (1978) "Policy of peace and our time." *Participation*, 2,3: 32-38.
SHARP, Walter R. (1950) "The scientific study of international conferences." *International Social Science Bulletin*, 2,1 (Spring): 104-116.
SHILS, Edward (1954) "Scientific community: thoughts after Hamburg." *Bulletin of the Atomic Scientists*, 10:5 (May): 151-154.
SKJELSBAEK, Kjell (1971) "The growth of international nongovernmental organization in the twentieth century." *International Organization*, 25,3 (Summer): 420-442.
SODDY, K. (1953) "International conferences and international nongovernmental organizations." *International Social Science Bulletin*, 5,2: 391-396.
STONE, Jeremy and A. Frederick SPILHAUS, Jr. (1980) "Scientists and international politics: a debate on linking scientific relations to Soviet actions." *Chemical and Engineering News*, 58,16 (21 April): 37-46.
STORER, Norman W. (1970) "The internationality of science and the nationality of scientists." *International Social Science Journal*, 22,1: 80-93.
TREASTER, Joseph B. (1979) "Homosexuals still fight U.S. immigration limits." *The New York Times* (12 August): 20.
TRENT, John E. (1978) "International research committees and political science." *Participation*, 2,2: 40-62.
UNESCO (1959) "The fourth world political science congress, Rome, 16-20 September 1958." *International Social Science Journal*, 11,2: 288-304.
———. (1953) "The technique of international conferences." *International Social Science Bulletin*, 5,2: 233-339.
———. (1951) "The world congress of political science." *International Social Science Bulletin*, 3,1 (Summer): 273-420.
———. (1950a) "The first world congress of political science: Zürich, 4-9 September 1950." *International Social Science Bulletin*, 2,4 (Winter): 545-547.
———. (1950b) "International Political Science Association." *International Social Science Bulletin*, 2,2 (Summer): 237-238.
———. (1949a) "International Political Science Association: summary report of the constituent conference held at UNESCO House, 12-16 September 1949." *International Social Science Bulletin*, 1,3-4: 81-85.
———. (1949b) "International political science conference 1949." *International Social Science Bulletin*, 1,1: 66-67.
———. (1949c) "The UNESCO project: methods in political science." *International Social Science Bulletin*, 1,1: 28-32.
UNION OF INTERGOVERNMENTAL ASSOCIATIONS [ed.] (1984) *Yearbook of International Organizations 1984/85* (21st ed). Munich: K. G. Saur Verlag.
URBAN, Michael E. (1980) "Communication." *PS*, 13:2 (Spring): 261-262.

WALKER, David (1986) "World archeology group in uproar over barring South African scholars." *The Chronicle of Higher Education*, 31:23 (19 February): 1+.

WEISS, Thomas G. and Robert S. JORDAN (1976) *The World Food Conference and Global Problem Solving*. New York: Praeger.

WILL, George F. (1978) "Such resolute political scientists." *The Washington Post* (14 September): 23.

WRIGHT, Quincy (1951) "The significance of the International Political Science Association." *International Social Science Bulletin*, 3,2 (Summer): 275-280.

Index

Afghanistan, as political issue, 116
Alger, Chadwick F., 7, 18
Alker, Hayward R., Jr., 36, 53
American Chemical Society (1977 in Cairo), 18
American Political Science Association: membership, 21–22; decision not to boycott Moscow World Congress, 47, 54–55, 105, 116 (*see also* Boycotts)
Angell, Robert Cooley, ix, 17, 129
Appadorai, Angadipuram, 53
Aron, Raymond, 53
Atelsek, Frank J., 140

Bacon, Francis, 41
Barber, Bernard, 26, 27, 121
Barents, Jan, 12–13, 48, 53
Becker, Howard S., 18
Bose, Nirmal, 36, 53
Boycotts, of ISCs, 16, 47, 54–55, 103–106, 116
Brezhnev, Leonid, message of welcome, 50
Bridel, Marcel, 53
Broadhead, Robert C., 18
Brogan, Denis W., 53
Brown, Archie, 50, 75

Cancian, Francesca M., 26
Capes, Mary, 1

Celikbas, Fethi, 53
Collins, H. M., 2
Communication: as goal of ISC, ix, 2, 68, 72, 77, 93–96, 120–122, 136–137; networking, 89–90, 91, 120, 136–137
Cost of ISCs (*see* ISCs *and* Site selection)
Crane, Diana, 5, 19

Data resources, need to develop, 138
Dependency theory, 18, 52
Deutsch, Karl W., 35, 45
Dickson, David, 16
Diffusion of research paradigms and results, 137–139
Disraeli, Benjamin, 78
Duverger, Maurice, 53

Evan, William M., 5, 6
Exupéry, Antoine de Saint, 131

Fighiera, Gian Carlo, 7, 8, 26
Frank, André Gunder, 53
Friedrich, Carl J., 44
Functional analysis, 1–4, 9–10, 24, 25–26

Ganon, Isaac, 53
Giniger, Henry, 118
Ginsburg, Alexander, 45–46 (*see also*

Soviet dissidents)
Global society, and ISCs, 17–18, 51–52
Goguel, François, 53
Gomberg, Irene L., 140
Goormaghtigh, John, 53

Hanson, Elizabeth C., 18
Hastad, Elis W., 53
Horowitz, Irving Louis, 18
Host country: functions of ISCs, 15–17, 50–51, 71, 127; cost of ISCs, x, 36, 51
Human rights, 16–17, 45–47, 116, 118

Inquiring community, 137
Integration, functional theories of, and ISCs, 2, 17, 52, 70, 97, 129–130
International nongovernmental organizations (INGOs), 4–9
International Political Science Association (IPSA): creation in 1949, 29–32; publications (review, abstracts, book series, newsletter), 29; and UNESCO, 30–31; world congresses, 32–34, 40–44, 48, 133–135 (*see also* Moscow World Congress, Paris, *and* Rio de Janeiro); research committees and study groups, 34–35, 136, 137; quality of world congresses, 125–126, 133–135
International professional associations, 4–6
International relations, structural theories of and ISCs, 2, 17
International scientific associations: functions of, 5–9; and ISCs, 7–9, 15
International scientific congresses (ISCs): and international communication, ix, x, 2, 77; costs, x, 20, 42, 135 (*see also* Site selection); functions of, 1–2, 9–19, 24, 48–49, 64–72, 132–139; for individuals, 10–13, 24, 48–49, 66, 67–69, 119–124 (*see also* Respondents); as medium for scientific communication, 11, 17–18, 29–30, 68, 72, 77, 93–96, 120–122, 136–137; as part of academic reward structure, 11, 120–124, 126–127, 131; for research organizations, 13–14, 49, 124; for scientific associations, 14–15, 49–50, 66, 68, 70–71, 124–127; for host country, 15–17, 50–51, 66, 68, 71, 127–128; for international system, 51–52, 128–132; participant characteristics, 10–11, 23–24, 48; politics and, 16, 101–102, 114–117, 127–132, 134; future directions, 132 (*see also* Moscow World Congress, Psychology, *and* Sociology)
Israeli visas, in 1979, 45, 116

Jagtenberg, Tom, 2
Johns Hopkins Center for Research in Scientific Communication, 11, 13, 77, 91–96, 99, 139
Jordan, Robert S., 27
Justice, 52

Kaplan, Abraham, 3
Kelman, Herbert C., 96
Khosla, H., 53
Knowledge, as power, 41 (*see also* Communication)
Kochen, Manfred, 137
Kriesberg, Louis, 6
Kuhn, Thomas, 26

Ladd, Everett Carll, Jr., 10, 48
Laponce, Jean A., 44
Lasswell, Harold D., 3
Levy, Marion J., Jr., 26
Lipset, Seymour Martin, 10, 48
Lodge, David, 12, 122
Ludz, Peter C., 36, 53
Lyons, Gene M., 7, 18

MacIver, Robert M., 3
MacPherson, C. B., 53
Mead, Margaret, 1
Mendes, Candido, 44
Menzel, Herbert, 18, 121
Merle, Marcel, 36, 53
Merritt, Richard L., 18, 36, 100
Merton, Robert K., 25, 26, 74, 128, 129
Meynaud, Jean, 5, 34, 53
Miller, James G., 140
Moscow World Congress (1979): xi, 2, 19, 32, 35-36; survey of participants, 19-25 (*see also* Respondents); choice of Moscow as site for meeting, 25, 36, 41, 42-47; attendees, 36-39, 48-49, 143-144; issue of dissidents, 45-47, 116, 118; possibility of boycott, 47, 50, 103-104; research organizations, 49, 124; disciplinary associations, 49-50, 66, 68, 70-71, 124-127; global society, 51-52, 128-132; Third World participants, 52, 60, 61, 88-90, 91, 131; participants' expectations and experiences, 78-84; impact on scholarly behavior, 90-96; problems emerging at conference, 115-117
Mulkay, Michael J., 2, 26

National disciplinary associations, and ISCs, 14-15
National governments, and ISCs, 15-17 (*see also* Host country)
National Science Board, report to U.S. Congress on status of science and technology, 11
Networking (*see* Communication)
Nuttin, Joseph R., 74-75, 95

Olympics, as political issue, 116
Orlov, Yuri Fyodorovich, 45 (*see also* Soviet dissidents)

Paris, as site of future IPSA world congress (1985), x, 32, 34, 109-111, 130, 135, 140-141
Peace, 17, 52
Pear, Robert, 54
Personal enrichment, 12-13
Philippart, André, 33, 34, 53
Polányi, Michael, 2
Politics: and Moscow World Congress, 45-47, 50-51, 102-109; impact on ISCs, 16, 101-102, 114-117, 127-132; of site selection, 36, 40-47
Price, Derek J. de Solla, 19
Professional growth, 11-12
Psychology, International Congress of, Moscow (1966), 11, 13, 91-96, 99, 139

Research organizations, and ISCs, 13-14, 49, 124
Respondents: registrants, 20-21, 57-59, 67-69, 73-74, 143-144; nonregistrants, 21-22, 58-59, 67-69, 73-74; professional status, 59-61, 62-63, 123, 169-170; international activity, 59-62, 62-63, 171-173; Third World participants, 60, 61, 88-90, 91; Western participants, 60, 61; reasons for attending professional meetings, 63-65; reasons for attending ISCs, 64-72; decision to attend, 72-73; political considerations for attending, 102-109; reasons for attending Moscow World Congress, 103, 119-124; expectations and experiences, 78-84; Soviet life, 84-87; attitude changes, 86, 96-97; post-congress networking, 87-90, 97-98; post-congress scholarly work, 90-93, 98-99; concerns raised, 93-96; views on Moscow as site, 106-109; Soviet propaganda, 112-114; as scientific elite, 119-120
Reynolds, P. A., 34

Rio de Janeiro, as site of future IPSA world congress (1982), 32, 34, 41, 44, 50, 109–111, 130, 131, 135
Rist, Ray C., 18
Robson, William A., 53
Rokkan, Stein, 44
Roosevelt, Curtis, 5
Rumanian Political Science Association, 43–44

Schaff, Adam, 53
Scientific consociation, 3–4, 9, 18, 26, 47, 132
Scientific discipline, definition, 3
Scientific knowledge, 27
Scohy, Michele, 33
Scully, Malcolm G., 54
Sebestik, Jutta, 23
Seltzer, Richard J., 17, 54
Semenov, Vadim S., 36, 53
Shakhnazarov, Georgii, 36, 53
Sharansky, Anatoly, 45, 46 (*see also* Soviet dissidents)
Sharp, Walter R., 27, 53
Shils, Edward, 2
Skjelsbaek, Kjell, 7
Site selection: financial considerations, x, 42, 135, 140–141; political considerations, 36, 40–47, 106–112, 134–135
Smirnov, William, 36, 100
Sociology, world congress of: Evian (1966), 11, 13, 91–96, 99, 139; Zürich (1950), 33–34
Soddy, K., 27
Soviet Union: Soviet Political Science Association, 44–45, 49–50, 75; dissidents, as political issue, 45–47, 54, 116, 118; participants' views of government and people, 84–87, 96–97; propaganda at Moscow World Congress, 103–104, 107–108, 112–114
Spilhaus, Frederick, Jr., 17, 54
Stone, Jeremy, 17, 54
Storer, Norman W., 27
Survey, 19–25, 145–168 (*see also* Respondents)

Technology transfer, ix, 18
Third World: needs of and ISCs, 18; and IPSA, 32; scholars, 52, 131 (*see also* Respondents); impact of ISCs, 72, 97–98, 125, 127, 130–131; networking with others, 88–90, 91
Toumanov, Vladimir, 44
Transnationalism, 5–6
Treaster, Joseph B., 54
Trent, John E., 33, 34, 54

UNESCO, and IPSA, 27, 30–31
Urban, Michael E., 100

Values: transnational, 6, 52; ISCs and exchange of, 130–132

Walker, David, 54, 117
Weiss, Thomas G., 27
Western Europe, international meetings in, 7–9
Will, George F., 55
Wright, Quincy, 32, 53

About the Book and the Authors

While there are many widely held assumptions about the impact of international scientific congresses (ISCs) on individual scientists, collective bodies, a particular branch of science, or even the establishment of world order, these assumptions have not previously been fully examined or tested empirically. Merritt and Hanson present here the results of their systematic investigation of the uses and consequences of ISCs. Deriving their data from a survey of political scientists from the nonsocialist countries who attended the 11th World Congress of the International Political Science Association in Moscow, as well as a control group of North American political scientists who did not attend the Moscow meetings, they explore the function of ISCs at both manifest and latent levels. Their results provide a solid basis for evaluating the costs versus the benefits of future scientific congresses.

Richard L. Merritt is professor of political science and communications at the University of Illinois, Urbana-Champaign, and served as program director of the 11th World Congress of the International Political Science Association. Elizabeth C. Hanson is associate professor of political science at the University of Connecticut.